NICOTEXT

The Student Cookbook

The Legal Text
Look here, dude, this book is ours. We made it, and we own it.
We therefore forbid you to do any of the following with it:
use the pages as toilet paper, use the book as a meal tray,
reproduce any part of this book without written permission from the
Publisher (that would be us).
If you ignore this warning we will get really, really upset with
you. That, and we'll put a snail on your eye while you're
sleeping. So, if you don't want a snail on your eye, do as we say!
Now, lean back and enjoy this here book we put together, just for you.

www.nicotext.com
info@nicotext.com

Fredrik Colting
Carl-Johan Gadd

Copyright ©NICOTEXT 2008 All rights reserved
ISBN 978-91-85449-11-8
Printed in USA

Index

Quick Guide

Food

Chicken Sandwich

1/2 dl (1/4 cup) flour
1 tsp salt
1/2 tsp black pepper
1/8 tsp cayenne
1 dl (1/3 cup) milk
1/4 dl (1/4 cup) vegetable oil
2 boneless chicken breasts
2 tbsp mayonaise
2 white sandwich rolls
2 tomato slices
2 lettuce leaves

Mix the flour, salt pepper and cayenne in a small bowl and
the milk in an other bowl. Heat oil in a skillet, dip all sides of the
chicken in the flour, then the milk, then the flour again. Fry until
golden brown, then turn and do the same on the other side.
The juices should run clear when poked with a knife. Spread mayo
on the rolls and fill each one with chicken, tomato and lettuce.

QUOTES QUOTES QUOTES

(Bobby wants plain toast, which isn't on the menu)
"-I'd like an omelet, plain, and a chicken salad sandwich on wheat toast,
no mayonnaise, no butter, no lettuce. And a cup of coffee.
-A #2, chicken salad sand. Hold the butter, the lettuce, the mayonnaise,
and a cup of coffee. Anything else?
-Yeah, now all you have to do is hold the chicken, bring me the toast,
give me a check for the chicken salad sandwich, and you haven't
broken any rules.
-You want me to hold the chicken, huh?
-I want you to hold it between your knees."

-Five Easy Pieces

Hot Rice with Prawns

1 onion
1 fresh chili pepper
1 piece of ginger, fresh
1 tablespoon olive oil
2 1/2 dl (1 cup) rice
450 g (1 lb) prawns, boiled
6 dl (2 1/2 cups) water
Pinch of salt
Tabasco

Peel and chop the onion. Grate the ginger.
Heat the olive oil in a pan and add rice.
Mix and fry for 5 minutes. Add onion, chili pepper and ginger.
Cover with water with salt.
Cook for 15-18 minutes.

Shell the prawns and cut in little pieces.
Add them to the rice.
Season with some drops of Tabasco and serve hot.

FACTS FACTS FACTS

Prawns are distinguished from the superficially similar shrimp
by their gill structure, which is branching in prawns
but is lamellar in shrimp.

Broccoli Casserole

6 dl (2 1/2 cups) rice, cooked
1 small jar Cheese Whiz
2 cans undiluted Cream of Mushroom Soup
2 1/2 dl (1 cup) onions, chopped
2 1/2 dl (1 cup) celery, chopped
2 packages broccoli, chopped

Sauté onions and celery until tender.
Mix Cheese Whiz with hot rice.
Mix soup, cooked broccoli, onion and celery with rice,
and bake uncovered in oven at 350 degree F.
for one hour.

QUOTES QUOTES QUOTES

"-I love broccoli. It's good for you.
-Newman, you wouldn't eat broccoli if it
was deep fried in chocolate sauce."

-Seinfeld

Bulgur, Lentil & Tofu Casserole
(VEGGIE)

1 1/2 dl (3/4 cup) lentils
7 dl (3 cups) vegetable stock
1 tsp rosemary
1 tsp tarragon
2 bay leaves
2 tbsp sesame oil
1 carrot, thinly sliced
4 garlic cloves, pressed
1 onion, chopped
1 package pressed tofu
1 1/2 dl (3/4 cup) corn
1 1/2 dl (3/4 cup) bulgur

Cook the bulgur, following instructions on package. In a large pot, cook the lentils in the stock along with all the spices for about 25 minutes. Remove the bay leaf.
While the lentils are cooking, heat the oil in a skillet.
Add the carrot, garlic, onion & tofu. Sauté for 5 minutes.
Add the corn & bulgur. Stir to mix well.
Remove from heat & add the lentils & cooking liquid.
Pour into a greased casserole and bake in oven at
350 degrees F for 20 minutes.

QUOTES QUOTES QUOTES

"-It's important to think. It's what separates us from lentils."

-The Fisher King

Enchiladas Old Style

900 g (2 lb) hamburger
1 can crushed tomatoes
2 onions, chopped
2 cloves garlic
1 can kidney beans, drained
4 tsp chili powder
1 tsp sugar
1 tsp each salt and pepper
1 bag corn tortillas
450 g (1 lb) cheese, grated
Oil for cooking tortillas

Brown hamburger, 1 chopped onion and garlic.
Add tomatoes, kidney beans and spices.
Let simmer for a couple of minutes. Heat oil, and cook tortillas to desired temperature. Drain on paper towels.
Put a tortilla on a plate, spoon mixture over it and sprinkle raw onion and cheese on sauce. Put on another tortilla and repeat with the layers as desired.

TRIVIA TRIVIA TRIVIA

"Estas no son enchiladas" means "These are not enchiladas" and is a phrase used in Mexico City to refer to something that is not simple.

Enchilada literally means "seasoned with chiles".

Hot Chicken Salad

5 dl (2 cups) cooked chicken, chopped
2 1/2 dl (1 cup) celery, chopped
1 dl (1/2 cup) cashews
2 1/2 dl (1 cup) mayonnaise
1 small onion, chopped
1/2 tsp salt
2 tbsp lemon juice
1 dl (1/2 cup) shredded Cheddar cheese
2 1/2 dl (1 cup) crushed potato chips

Heat oven to 400 degrees F (200 degrees C).
In a medium bowl, mix chicken, celery, cashews, mayonnaise, onion, salt and lemon juice. Transfer the mixture to a casserole dish, then top with shredded cheese and potato chips. Bake uncovered for 20 minutes, or until heated through and bubbly.

FUN FUN FUN

A chicken can be hypnotized, or put into a trance, by holding its head down against the ground and continuously drawing a line along the ground with a stick or a finger, starting at its beak and extending straight outward in front of the chicken. If the chicken is hypnotized in this manner, it will remain immobile for somewhere between 15 seconds to 30 minutes, continuing to stare at the line.

Chicken Nachos

2 chicken breasts, chopped
2 tbsp vegetable oil
1 tsp cayenne pepper
1 package corn tortilla chips
1 package shredded Mexican-style cheese blend
1 can diced green chilies, drained

In a medium bowl, stir together the chicken, vegetable oil,
and cayenne pepper.
Let stand for 15 minutes, or longer if desired.
Heat a skillet over medium-high heat.
Add the chicken mixture, and fry until chicken is no longer pink.
Remove from heat, and set aside.
Preheat oven to 325 degrees F (165 degrees C). Spread a thin
layer of tortilla chips in a 23x33 cm (9x13 inch) baking dish.
Sprinkle 1/4 of the chicken, 1/4 of the chiles, and 1/4 of the cheese
over the chips. Repeat layers ending with cheese on the top.
Bake for 15 to 20 minutes in the preheated oven, until
the cheese is melted and everything is heated through.
Serve with your favorite nacho toppings.

TRIVIA TRIVIA TRIVIA

International Day of the Nacho is annually celebrated on October 21.

Nachos were created in Piedras Negras, Coahuila, Mexico.

Chicken
Caesar Salad

450 g (1 lb) chicken breasts, cut into wide strips
1 1/2 tsp lemon & pepper seasoning salt
1 tsp garlic powder
1/2 dl (1/4 cup) olive oil
2 tbsp white wine vinegar
1 tsp Dijon-style mustard
1/2 tsp Worcestershire sauce
1 head lettuce, shredded
2 1/2 dl (1 cup) garlic-flavored croutons
1/2 dl (1/4 cup) grated Parmesan cheese

Toss chicken with lemon & pepper seasoning and garlic powder.
Heat oil in nonstick skillet over medium-high heat. Add seasoned
chicken and cook 4 to 5 minutes or until thoroughly cooked.
Place vinegar, mustard and Worcestershire in small bowl and
beat with fork to combine. Stir into reserved chicken.
Place lettuce in large salad bowl. Add chicken, croutons, and
cheese. Toss gently and sprinkle with additional grated cheese.

QUOTES QUOTES QUOTES

"-It seems to me the only thing you've learned is
that Caesar is a "salad dressing dude"."

-Bill & Ted's Excellent Adventure

Apple Salad with Lemon Dressing

Salad:
5 apples, peeled, cored and cut into bite-size pieces
3 1/2 dl (1 1/2 cup) raisins
2 1/2 dl (1 cup) pecans, chopped
3 1/2 dl (1 1/2 cup) celery, chopped

Dressing:
6 tbsp salad oil
1 1/2 dl (3/4 cup) honey
2 tbsp poppy seeds
1 dl (1/2 cup) frozen lemonade concentrate

In a large bowl, mix the apples, raisins, pecans and celery. In a separate bowl, whisk the oil, honey, poppy seeds and lemonade concentrate. Add the dressing to the apple mixture and mix thoroughly.

FACTS FACTS FACTS

45 million metric tons of apples are grown worldwide. China produces almost half of this total. Argentina is the second leading producer, with more than 15% of the world production.

In the United States, more than 60% of all the apples sold commercially are grown in Washington state.

BLT Salad with Avocado Dressing

Dressing:
1 ripe avocado, peeled, mashed
1 dl (1/2 cup) sour cream
1/2 dl (1/4 cup) milk
1/2 dl (1/4 cup) mayonnaise
1 tbsp lemon juice
1/4 tsp garlic salt
2 drops hot pepper sauce

Salad:
7 dl (3 cups) lettuce, shredded
3 tomatoes, sliced
200 g (1/2 lb) bacon, crisp cooked, crumbled
1 1/2 dl (3/4 cup) croutons,

In small bowl, combine all dressing ingredients; beat until smooth.
Cover and refrigerate for several hours to blend flavors.
At serving time, toss salad ingredients in large salad bowl.
Serve with dressing.

QUOTES QUOTES QUOTES

"-Uh, Hello, room service? I'd like some bacon,
a couple of cokes, and a bunch of whores."

-Beavis and Butt-Head

Couscous Salad
(VEGGIE)

5 dl (2 cups) couscous, cooked
1 scallion, sliced
1 cucumber, peeled and diced
1 tomato, diced
1 bell pepper, diced
1/2 dl (1/4 cup) mozzarella
1 clove garlic, minced
1 tbsp olive oil
2 tbsp red wine
Basil, oregano and pepper to taste

In a small bowl, whisk together oil and vinegar. Mix in garlic and scallion and seasonings and set aside. Mix cooled couscous and vegetables. Add cheese and mix gently. Drizzle in dressing. Refrigerate until serving.

TRIVIA TRIVIA TRIVIA

Couscous originates from Northern Africa where another popular dish is "stuffed camel", the largest item on a menu in the world. You simply stuff the camel with one whole lamb, stuffed with 20 whole chickens, stuffed with 60 eggs along with rice, nuts salt and pepper to taste.

Spinach Salad

450 g (1 lb) spinach
1/2 dl (1/4 cup) almonds, sliced
1 can mandarin oranges
4 slices bacon, cooked and crumbled

Dressing:
1/2 dl (1/4 cup) sugar
1 dl (1/3 cup) white wine vinegar
1/4 tsp salt
2 tbsp oil

Combine spinach, almonds, oranges and bacon.
In small bowl, mix dressing ingredients until sugar is dissolved.
Pour over salad and serve.

QUOTES QUOTES QUOTES

"-So you don't like spinach?
-I hates it. "

"-Children. They're just smaller versions of us you know, but I'm not so
crazy about me in the first place, so why would I want one of them?"

-Popeye

Chicken Pasta Salad

4 dl (1 3/4 cups) chicken broth
1 dl (1/2 cup) mayonnaise
1/2 dl (1/4 cup) sour cream
1/2 dl (1/4 cup) Parmesan cheese, grated
1 tsp dried dill weed
7 dl (3 cups) corkscrew pasta, cooked
2 1/2 dl (1 cup) cherry tomatoes, halved
2 1/2 dl (1 cup) frozen peas, cooked
1 dl (1/2 cup) mushrooms, sliced
1 red onion, minced
5 dl (2 cups) cooked chicken, cubed

Mix broth, mayonnaise, cheese and dill. Toss in pasta, tomatoes, peas, mushrooms, onion, chicken and broth mixture until evenly coated. Serve on a bed of lettuce.

FACTS FACTS FACTS

A short guide to pastas:

Conchiglie - sea shell shaped
Farfalle - bow tie shaped
Rotelle - wagon wheel shaped
Campanelle - small cones
Fiori – flower shaped
Radiatori - shaped like radiators
Quadrefiore - square with rippled edges
Maltagliati - flat roughly cut triangles

Tortellini Salad with Caesar Dressing

250 g (9 oz) cheese tortellini
5 dl (2 cups) broccoli florets
1 tomato, chopped

Dressing:
1 dl (1/2 cup) sour cream
1 dl (1/3 cup) water
1/2 dl (1/4 cup) white wine vinegar
1 package dry Caesar salad dressing mix

Cook tortellini according to package directions. Add broccoli during last 30 seconds of cooking. Rinse with cold water and drain. Mix ingredients for dressing in small bowl. Combine cooked pasta, broccoli and tomato in large bowl.
Pour 1 dl (1/2 cup) dressing over salad, tossing lightly to coat. Serve with additional dressing if desired.

TRIVIA TRIVIA TRIVIA

The absolute true story of how tortellini was invented.
Venus and Jupiter were set to meet one night and after Venus had checked into an inn, she waited for Jupiter on the bed. The chef found out, went to her room and peeked through the keyhole, where he saw only her navel. Overcome by the sight, the chef was so inspired that he created a stuffed pasta resembling it.

Black Bean Salad

2 1/2 dl (1 cup) corn
2 1/2 dl (1 cup) jicama, diced
1 1/2 dl (3/4 cup) chopped tomato
2 green onions, sliced
2 cans black beans

Dressing:
1/2 dl (1/4 cup) red wine vinegar
2 tbsp vegetable oil
1/2 tsp chili powder
1/4 tsp ground cumin
1 clove garlic, crushed

Toss all salad ingredients in large bowl.
Mix ingredients for dressing in another bowl.
Combine and refrigerate for 1 hour before serving.

QUOTES QUOTES QUOTES

"-Bachelor number 3, what's your name and where d'you come from?
-Um, well I'm... Number 3. And I've come... from my dressing room.
-Aww, bless his little cotton socks! I meant, where are you from,
what's your name?
-Er, Bean.
-What's your first name?
-(pause) Mister."

-Mr. Bean

Spinach Pie
(VEGGIE)

1 frozen pie crust
100 g (4 oz) mushrooms
1 tsp vegetable oil
2 packages spinach soufflés, thawed
200 g (8 oz) mozzarella cheese, shredded

Slice and sauté mushrooms in oil. Place in bottom of pie shell.
Sprinkle 1/3 of the cheese over the mushrooms and top
with spinach soufflés and the remainder of the cheese.
Bake in 350 degrees F for about 45 minutes
or until the cheese is completely melted.
Let cool for 10-15 minutes before serving.

FACTS FACTS FACTS

There are two American localities, Alma, Arkansas and Crystal City, Texas,
that claim to be the "Spinach Capital of the World."
In Crystal City stands a statue of Popeye. Thanks to that cartoon,
the consumption of spinach in the United States increased with a third.

Beef Tortellini Soup

450 g (1 lb) ground beef
800 g (28 oz) pureed tomatoes, canned
300 g (10 oz) French onion soup, canned
1 package frozen green beans
1 package fresh cheese tortellini
1 tbsp dried basil leaves
1 zucchini

Brown ground beef in a pot, stirring frequently until beef is well browned. Add tomatoes, onion soup, green beans, tortellini, basil and 8 dl (3 1/2 cups) water. Bring to boil over high heat, then reduce heat to medium.
Cover and cook another 10 minutes, stirring occasionally.
Add zucchini, and cook uncovered for another 10 minutes until zucchini and tortellini are tender.

QUOTES QUOTES QUOTES

"-So the meatloaf is essentially ground beef and bread crumbs?
And ground beef is essentially nothing more than dead cow?"

-3rd Rock from the Sun

Meatball Minestrone Soup

2 cans chicken broth
1 can beef broth
1 bag frozen mixed vegetables
1 bag frozen meatballs
1 can stewed tomatoes
1 dl (1/2 cup) macaroni noodles
1 can kidney beans
1 1/2 tbsp dried Italian seasoning
6 tbsp Parmesan cheese, grated

Heat chicken and beef broth in a pot. Add the still-frozen vegetables and meatballs. Add the tomatoes and macaroni. Bring it to a boil. Rinse and drain the kidney beans and add to the pot along with Italian seasoning. Reduce heat to medium. Stir frequently until the macaroni is tender, about 6 to 7 minutes more. Serve with Parmesan cheese.

QUOTES QUOTES QUOTES

"-Mamma Mia! The cruel meatball of war has rolled onto our laps and ruined our white pants of peace!"

-Futurama

Tex Mex Corn Chowder

200 g (1/2 lb) ground mild sausage
1/2 dl (1/4 cup) chopped onion
2 cloves garlic, minced
5 dl (2 cups) milk
1 can cream of chicken soup
2 1/2 dl (1 cup) sweet corn
2 tomatoes, chopped
1 small can chopped green chilies
2 tbsp cilantro, minced
1/4 tsp ground red pepper
2 1/2 dl (1 cup) Monterey Jack cheese, shredded

In a pot, cook ground sausage, onion, and garlic until sausage is no longer pink. Stir in milk, cream of chicken, corn, chopped tomato, green chilies, cilantro and ground red pepper.
Bring to boil. Reduce heat and let simmer, for approximately 8 to 10 minutes, stirring often.
Add cheese and let it melt.
Serve at once.

FUN FUN FUN

Newport, Rhode Island's Great Chowder Cook-Off, held each year since 1981, is the world's largest and oldest chowder competition.

Beef Noodle Soup

2 tbsp oil
200 g (1/2 lb) boneless beef steak, cut into thin strips
1/2 dl (1/4 cup) green onion, chopped
1 tbsp all-purpose flour
3 cans condensed chicken broth
7 dl (3 cups) water
5 dl (2 cups) egg noodles, cooked

Heat oil in 3-quart saucepan. Add beef and cook until brown.
Add onion and cook until tender. Stir in flour.
Add chicken broth and water. Heat to boiling,
stirring occasionally. Let simmer for about 5 minutes.
Stir in noodles and heat before serving.

TRIVIA TRIVIA TRIVIA

When composer Giuseppe Verdi (1813-1901)
needed inspiration, he had a bowl of noodle soup.

Parmesan Rice

2 tbsp butter
7 dl (3 cups) rice, cooked
100 g (4 oz) mushrooms, chopped
1/2 dl (1/4 cup) peas, defrosted
1 dl (1/2 cup) parmesan cheese, grated

Melt butter in large skillet over medium heat.
Add rice, mushrooms and peas.
Cook for about 5 minutes.
Add parmesan, stir until well blended and serve.

FACTS FACTS FACTS

Cheeses Around the World:

Yak cheese – Nepal
Bokmakiri cheese – South Africa
Prince-Jean cheese – Belgium
Danish Blue cheese – Denmark
Halloumi - Cyprus
Ardrahan cheese – Ireland
Bel paese cheese – Italy
Manchego cheese – Spain
Emmental - Switzerland

Chinese Fried Rice

1 dl (1/2 cup) cooked ham, chicken or pork, diced
2 tbsp oil
100 g (3 oz) mushrooms, sliced
9 1/2 dl (4 cups) rice, cooked
1 green onion, chopped
2 tbsp soy sauce
1 egg, beaten

Brown meat in hot oil.
Add all ingredients, except egg.
Stir frequently and cook for 10 minutes over low heat.
Add egg and cook 5 more minutes before serving.

QUOTES QUOTES QUOTES

"-Flied lice? It's fried rice, you plick."

-Lethal Weapon 4

Bacon Cheeseburger Rice

450 g (1 lb) ground beef
4 dl (1 3/4 cups) water
1 1/2 dl (2/3 cups) BBQ sauce
1 tbsp mustard
2 tsp dried minced onion
1/2 tsp pepper
5 dl (2 cups) uncooked instant rice
2 1/2 dl (1 cup) cheddar, shredded
1 dl (1/3 cup) dill pickles, chopped
5 bacon strips, cooked and crumbled

In a large saucepan, cook beef until brown. Add water, BBQ sauce, mustard, onion and pepper. Bring to a boil and stir in the rice. Reduce heat, cover and simmer for 5 minutes. Sprinkle with pickles, bacon and cheese before serving.

TRIVIA TRIVIA TRIVIA

At the start of 2005, the largest commercially available cheeseburger was "Ye Olde 96er" from Denny's Beer Barrel Pub in Clearfield, Pennsylvania. The total mass of the sandwich was eleven pounds.
Competitions involving the "96er" were held, but no customer was able to finish the it within the challenge's time limit of three hours, until the beginning of 2005, when Kate Stelnick, a 115 pound college student from Princeton, New Jersey, finished her colossal cheeseburger in two hours and 54 minutes, becoming the first diner to win the challenge.

Tex-Mex Rice Meal

450 g (1 lb) ground beef, browned
1 onion, chopped
1 dl (1/3 cup) oil
2-3 tbsp garlic, chopped
800 g (28 oz) diced tomatoes, canned
1 can corn
1 can black beans
1 small can green chilies
6 dl (2 1/2 cups) water
1 teaspoon salt
7 dl (3 cups) instant rice

Sauté onion in oil until soft, then add garlic.
Pour in canned vegetables. Add water and salt, bring to a boil.
Add instant rice. Cook until rice is tender and most of the moisture
is absorbed, about 10-15 minutes. Add ground beef and serve.

FACTS FACTS FACTS

"Forbidden rice" is a short-grained heirloom rice that is black when
raw and dark purple when cooked. The name comes from a legend
that claims the rice was reserved for emperors in ancient China
because of its nutrition and rarity.

Pasta Primavera

1 package cheese tortellini
2 1/2 dl (1 cup) hot water
5 dl (2 cups) broccoli florets
2 1/2 dl (1 cup) tomatoes, quartered
2 1/2 dl (1 cup) carrots, sliced
2 1/2 dl (1 cup) feta cheese, crumbled
2 1/2 dl (1 cup) Italian salad dressing
1/2 dl (1/4 cup) green onions, sliced

Prepare tortellini according to package directions and let cool in refrigerator. Boil water in a saucepan and add broccoli florets. Cook for 30 seconds. Remove tortellini from refrigerator and place in a large bowl. Combine tortellini, broccoli, tomatoes, carrots, feta, salad dressing and onions. Stir gently and serve.

QUOTES QUOTES QUOTES

"-I don't know. I just want to... get healthy. I would like to start taking better care of myself. I'd like to start eating healthier - I don't want all that pasta. I would like to start eating like Japanese food."

-Lost in Translation

Potato and Spinach Frittata

1 tbsp olive oil
7 dl (3 cups) frozen potatoes
1/2 dl (1/4 cups) red peppers, chopped
1 clove garlic, minced
5 dl (2 cups) spinach leaves, torn
6 eggs
1/2 dl (1/4 cup) milk
3/4 tsp salt
1/2 tsp dried basil leaves
1/4 tsp pepper
3 1/2 dl (1 1/2 cups) Swiss cheese, shredded

Fry potatoes, red bell pepper and garlic in oil, until potatoes are golden brown. Add spinach. Cook and stir 1 to 2 minutes or until spinach is wilted. In a small bowl, beat together eggs, milk, salt, basil and pepper until blended. Stir in cheese and pour into skillet. Cover and cook 6 to 8 minutes or until top surface of egg is set.

TRIVIA TRIVIA TRIVIA

Know your potatoes:

Russet Burbank
Yellow Finn
Red Gold
German Butterball
Maris Piper
International Kidney
Golden Wonder
Pink Fir Apple
Jersey Benies

Parmesan Mashed Potatoes

700 g (1 1/2 lb) potatoes, peeled and cubed
1 garlic clove, crushed
1 dl (1/3 cup) milk
3 tbsp grated Parmesan cheese
3/4 tsp salt

Boil potatoes until soft.
Add garlic and mash until smooth.
Add milk, cheese, and salt.
Beat until light and fluffy.

QUOTES QUOTES QUOTES

"-I can't even eat. The food keeps touching. I like military plates.
I'm a military man, I want a military meal. I want my string beans to be
quarantined! I like a little fortress around my mashed potatoes so the
meatloaf doesn't invade my mashed potatoes and cause mixing in my
plate! I HATE IT when food touches! I'm a military man, you understand
that? And don't let your food touch either, please?"

-Toys

Chicken Strips

4 chicken breasts
1 egg, beaten
1 tbsp Dijon mustard
1 tbsp water
1/2 dl (1/4 cup) flour
1 1/2 dl (3/4 cup) dry seasoned bread crumbs
2 tbsp vegetable oil
2 tbsp butter
1/2 tbsp lemon pepper seasoning
Salt to taste

Cut each chicken breast in 6 pieces. In a small bowl, mix egg, mustard and water together. Mix flour and lemon pepper on a plate. Place the breadcrumbs on a separate plate. Dip the strips in the flour, then the egg and the breadcrumbs. In a skillet, add the oil and butter. Brown chicken in skillet on all sides (about six minutes total). Season with salt and serve with dipping sauce.

FACTS FACTS FACTS

Chickens are the most common bird in the world.
The population in 2003 was 24 billion, according
to the Firefly Encyclopedia of Birds.

Garlic Chicken

3 tbsp butter
4 skinless, boneless chicken breast halves
2 tsp garlic powder
1 tsp seasoning salt
1 tsp onion powder

Melt butter in a large skillet over medium high heat.
Add chicken and sprinkle with garlic powder, seasoning salt and
onion powder. Sautee about 10 to 15 minutes on each side,
or until chicken is cooked through and juices run clear.

TRIVIA TRIVIA TRIVIA

In the United States, Gilroy, California promotes itself
as "Garlic Capital of the World", and hosts the
Gilroy Garlic Festival every summer.

BBQ Chicken Pizza

1 pre-baked pizza crust
1 dl (1/2 cup) barbecue sauce
1 dl (1/2 cup) grilled chicken, diced
1/2 dl (1/4 cup) red bell pepper, chopped
1/2 dl (1/4 cup) green bell pepper, chopped
1/2 dl (1/4 cup) red onion, chopped
2 1/2 dl (1 cup) Monterey Jack cheese, shredded

Preheat oven to 450 degrees F (230 degrees C). Grease cookie sheet and place pizza crust on it. Spread with barbecue sauce. Scatter chicken over top. Sprinkle evenly with red pepper, green pepper and onion. Cover with cheese. Bake in oven for 10 to 12 minutes, or until cheese is melted.

TRIVIA TRIVIA TRIVIA

In Australia, the barbeque, or "Barbie", is an important cultural expression of the outdoor lifestyle. Australian celebrity Paul Hogan is famous for his phrase "whack a couple of shrimps on the barbie for ya".
Australians will cook basic meats such as snags, chops and steaks, accompanied by beer, conversation and "a kick of the footy".

Cheeseburger Pizza

200 g (1/2 lb) ground beef
1 onion, chopped
2 1/2 dl (1 cup) Thousand Island salad dressing
1 pre-baked pizza crust
1/2 tsp seasoning salt
2 1/2 dl (1 cup) American cheese, shredded
5 dl (2 cups) lettuce, shredded
1 tomato, chopped
Dill pickle slices

Cook ground beef in a skillet until evenly browned. Season with seasoning salt. Preheat the oven to 450 degrees F (230 degrees C). Spread salad dressing on the pizza crust. Top with a layer of ground beef and onion. Sprinkle shredded cheese on top. Bake for 8 to 10 minutes, until cheese is melted. Allow pizza to cool for about 5 minutes, then slice into wedges and top with lettuce, tomato and pickles.

FACTS FACTS FACTS

The trademark for the name "cheeseburger" was awarded
in 1935 to Louis Ballast of the Humpty Dumpty
Drive-In in Denver, Colorado.

Canadian Bacon Macaroni and Cheese

2 1/2 dl (1 cup) elbow macaroni
6 strips Canadian-style bacon
2 tbsp margarine
2 1/2 tbsp all-purpose flour
2 1/2 dl (1 cup) canned tomatoes
2 1/2 dl (1 cup) Cheddar cheese, shredded

Cook macaroni until al dente. Fry bacon and place on paper towel to drain. Cut into bite size pieces. Melt margarine in a large saucepan over medium-low heat. Stir in flour, then tomatoes and wait for sauce to thicken, stirring occasionally. Stir in cheese and cooked macaroni and bacon and heat through, until cheese is melted.

QUOTES QUOTES QUOTES

"-There's a time to think, and a time to act.
And this, gentlemen, is no time to think."

-Canadian Bacon

Chicken Pesto Pizza

1 dl (1/2 cup) pesto basil sauce
1 pre-baked pizza crust
5 dl (2 cups) chicken breast strips, cooked
1 jar artichoke hearts, drained
1 dl (1/2 cup) Mozzarella cheese, shredded

Preheat oven to 450 degrees F (230 degrees C).
Spread pesto sauce over the pizza crust. Arrange chicken pieces and artichoke hearts over the sauce, and sprinkle with cheese. Bake for 8 to 10 minutes until cheese is melted and lightly browned at the edges.

TRIVIA TRIVIA TRIVIA

In Hong Kong, Pizza Hut customers may choose to have their pizzas dressed with Thousand Island dressing instead of tomato sauce.

In India , pizza toppings include curry and other traditional sauces or chunks of tandoori chicken.

In Japan, pizza toppings may include corn, diced potatoes, scrambled eggs, mayonnaise, Camembert cheese, curry sauce, and various kinds of seafood.

Chili Dog Casserole

2 cans chili with beans
1 package beef frankfurters
10 flour tortillas
1 package Cheddar cheese, shredded

Preheat oven to 425 degrees F (220 degrees C).
Spread 1 can of chili and beans in the bottom of a baking dish.
Roll up franks inside tortillas and place in baking dish, seam side down, on top of chili and beans. Top with remaining can of chili and beans, and sprinkle with cheese.
Cover baking dish with aluminum foil, and bake in oven at 425 degrees F (220 degrees C)
for 30 minutes. Serve.

QUOTES QUOTES QUOTES

"-Why did the man put a sweater on his hot dog?
Because it was a chili dog. Wokka wokka wokka."

-Muppet Babies

Cowboy Hash

450 g (1 lb) ground beef
1 tbsp vegetable oil
5 dl (2 cups) corn
8 dl (3 1/2 cups) canned beans

Heat oil in a large skillet over medium high heat. Sautee ground
beef until browned. Stir in corn and beans, cover and let simmer
for 10 minutes. Serve over hot cooked rice

FACTS FACTS FACTS

The Club des Hashischins was a Parisian society dedicated to the
exploration of drug-induced experiences, notably with hashish.
It was active from about 1844 to 1849 and counted the literary and
intellectual elite of Paris among its members, including Dr. Jacques-Joseph
Moreau, Théophile Gautier, Charles Baudelaire, Gérard de Nerval, Eugène
Delacroix and Alexandre Dumas.

Cajun Jambalaya

2 tsp olive oil
2 chicken breasts, cut into bite-size pieces
200 g (8 oz) kielbasa, diced
1 onion, diced
1 green bell pepper, diced
1 dl (1/2 cup) celery, diced
3 garlic cloves, chopped
1/4 tsp cayenne pepper
1/2 tsp onion powder
Salt and ground black pepper to taste
5 dl (2 cups) uncooked white rice
9 1/2 dl (4 cups) chicken stock
3 bay leaves
2 tsp Worcestershire sauce
1 tsp hot pepper sauce

Sautee chicken and kielbasa in a large pot until lightly browned (about 5 minutes). Stir in onion, bell pepper, celery and garlic. Season with cayenne, onion powder, salt and pepper. Cook 5 minutes, or until onion is tender and translucent. Add rice, then stir in chicken stock and bay leaves. Bring to a boil, reduce heat, and let simmer for 20 minutes, or until rice is tender. Stir in the Worcestershire sauce and hot pepper sauce before serving.

QUOTES QUOTES QUOTES

"-That's fuckin' blasphemy. Elvis wasn't a Cajun."

-The Commitments

Eggplant Burgers
(VEGGIE)

1 eggplant, peeled and sliced into 2 cm (3/4 inch) rounds
1 tbsp margarine
6 slices Monterey Jack cheese
6 hamburger buns, split
6 leaves lettuce
6 slices tomato
1/2 onion, sliced
1 dl (1/2 cup) dill pickle slices
Ketchup
Mayonnaise
Prepared yellow mustard

Place the eggplant slices on a plate, and cook in the microwave for about 5 minutes, or until the centers are cooked.
Melt margarine in a large skillet over medium-high heat.
Fry eggplant slices until lightly toasted on each side, and place one slice of cheese onto each one. Cook until cheese has melted. Place eggplant on hamburger buns, and top with lettuce, tomato, onion, and pickles, ketchup, mayonnaise and mustard, if desired.

TRIVIA TRIVIA TRIVIA

An egg cannot be cracked between the buttocks due to the equal distribution of force on the eggs surface area.

An ostrich egg can make omelets for ten people, and takes forty-five minutes of boiling to harden through.

Beef Macaroni and Cheese

5 dl (2 cups) elbow macaroni
450 g (1 lb) ground beef
1 can condensed tomato soup
1 can tomato juice
1 can corn
3 1/2 dl (1 1/2 cups) Mozzarella cheese, shredded

Boil pasta for 8 to 10 minutes or until cooked al dente.
In a skillet over medium heat, brown the ground beef until no pink shows. Combine macaroni, beef, tomato soup, tomato juice and corn in the pot. Heat through and stir in cheese.

QUOTES QUOTES QUOTES

"-Bless this highly nutritious microwavable macaroni and cheese dinner and the people who sold it on sale. Amen."

-Home Alone

Ground Turkey Stroganoff

1 package egg noodles
1 tbsp vegetable oil
450 g (1 lb) ground turkey
1 tbsp onion, minced
1 cube chicken bouillon
1 can cream of mushroom soup
1 dl (1/2 cup) water
1 tbsp paprika
Salt to taste

Cook egg noodles in a pot for 6 to 8 minutes, until al dente.
Cook turkey and onion in a skillet until brown and onion is tender.
Mix in the crumbled bouillon. Stir the cream of mushroom soup
and water into the skillet. Cook and stir until heated through.
Season with paprika and salt.
Serve over the cooked egg noodles.

QUOTES QUOTES QUOTES

"-If I had my way, I'd never work. I'd just stay home all day, watch Scarface
fifty times, eat a turkey sandwich, and have sex all fucking day. Then I'd
dress up like a clown, and surprise kids at schools. Then I'd take a dump
in the back of a movie theater, and just wait until somebody sat in it.
Hear it squish. That's funny to me."

-Chappelle's Show

Sausage and Peppers Mafia Style

200 g (1 8 ounce package) thin spaghetti
4 links sweet Italian sausage
5 bell peppers, cut into strips
1 clove garlic, minced
1/2 dl (1/4 cup) olive oil
1/2 tsp dried oregano
1/2 tsp dried basil
Salt and pepper to taste
1/2 dl (1/4 cup) leaf parsley, minced
Freshly grated Parmesan cheese to taste

Cook spaghetti until al dente, about 5 minutes.
Slice sausages lengthwise, and remove the casings.
Brown sausages in a large skillet over medium-high heat with
a drizzle of the olive oil. Remove sausages and add bell peppers,
garlic, oregano and basil, and drizzle with the remaining olive oil.
Sauté until peppers are tender. Toss the mixture with the drained
spaghetti until well blended, and season with salt and pepper to
taste. Transfer to a serving platter, and arrange the sausages on
the top. Garnish with Italian parsley and Parmesan cheese.

Watch out for:

The Italian Cosa Nostra, the Japanese Yakuza, the Chinese Triads,
the Indian Thuggee, the Russian Mafia and the Mexican Mafia.

Potato Curry

3 tbsp butter
1 tsp cumin seeds
1 tsp turmeric
1 tsp ground coriander
1 tsp salt
1/2 tsp mustard seed
1/2 tsp ground cayenne pepper
6 medium potatoes, peeled and diced
5 dl (2 cups) water
2 1/2 dl (1 cup) yogurt
1 1/2 dl (2/3 cup) frozen green peas

Heat the butter in a skillet over medium heat, and mix in the cumin, turmeric, coriander, salt, mustard seed, and cayenne pepper. Place potatoes in skillet, and stir to evenly coat with butter. Cook 10 minutes, stirring often. Pour water into the skillet. Reduce heat to low, and simmer 30 minutes, until potatoes are tender. Mix the yogurt and peas into the saucepan. Continue cooking until heated through. Serve.

TRIVIA TRIVIA TRIVIA

Some people are curry addicts. A number of studies have claimed that the reaction of pain receptors to the hotter ingredients in curries leads to the body's release of endorphins and, combined with the reaction to the variety of spices and flavours, a natural high is achieved that causes subsequent cravings, and the desire to move on to hotter curries.

Tuna Casserole

1 package macaroni and cheese
1 can condensed cream of mushroom soup
1 can tuna, drained
1 can peas, drained

Prepare macaroni and cheese according to package directions.
Stir in the cream of mushroom soup, tuna and peas.
Mix well, and heat until bubbly.

FACTS FACTS FACTS

Tuna have been measured swimming
at 77 kilometers per hour.

Now that's a fast fish!

Turkey and Rice

7 dl (3 cups) water
3 1/2 dl (1 1/2 cups) uncooked rice
1 tbsp cooking oil
2 1/2 dl (1 cup) green bell pepper, chopped
2 stalks celery, chopped
1 yellow onion, chopped
450 g (1 lb) boneless turkey breast, cut into 1 inch cubes
400 g (1 14.5 oz) can stewed tomatoes, drained

Cook rice in a saucepan for 20 minutes.
Meanwhile, sauté bell pepper, celery and onion in oil until tender,
about 2 to 3 minutes. Add turkey, and continue to sauté until
turkey loses its outer pink color. Stir in tomatoes and cover.
Continue to simmer, stirring occasionally, until turkey is
cooked through. Serve over hot cooked rice.

FACTS FACTS FACTS

Turkeys are so stupid that they can drown if they look
up in the sky when it rains.

Angel Hair Pasta Salad

2 packages angel hair pasta
200 g (1/2 lb) cooked shrimp
1 1/2 dl (3/4 cup) green onions, chopped
3 1/2 dl (1 1/2 cups) ranch-style salad dressing

Cook the pasta according to package directions.
Mix together pasta, shrimp, green onions and dressing.
Work the shrimp into the pasta with your hands before serving.

FACTS FACTS FACTS

Angel names:

Azrael
Chamuel
Jophiel
Malik
Metatron
Nakir and Munkar
Obbieuth
Phanuel
Raziel
Remiel
Sandalphon
Shamsiel
Zadkiel

Baked Salmon Fillets Dijon

4 (100 g / 4 oz) fillets salmon
3 tbsp Dijon mustard
Salt and pepper to taste
1/2 dl (1/4 cup) dry bread crumbs
1/2 dl (1/4 cup) butter, melted

Preheat oven to 400 degrees F (200 degrees C). Line a shallow baking pan with aluminum foil. Place salmon skin-side down on foil. Spread a thin layer of mustard on the top of each fillet, and season with salt and pepper. Top with bread crumbs, then drizzle with melted butter. Bake for 15 minutes, or until salmon flakes easily with a fork. Serve with rice and veggies.

QUOTES QUOTES QUOTES

"-Marijuana is not a drug. I used to suck dick for coke.
Now that's an addiction. You ever suck some dick for marijuana?"

-Half Baked

Salmon Pasta

1 package spaghetti
1 1/2 tbsp olive oil
2 1/2 dl (1 cup) onions, chopped
3 green onions, chopped
2 tbsp basil pesto
2 cans salmon, drained and flaked
1 dl (1/2 cup) Parmesan cheese

Cook pasta for 8 to 10 minutes, or until al dente.
Heat olive oil in a skillet and sauté onions, green onions, and
pesto. Cook until tender. Mix in salmon, and cook until heated
through. Stir in 1/2 the Parmesan cheese, and continue cooking
5 minutes. Toss with the cooked pasta, and sprinkle with remaining
Parmesan cheese to serve.

FACTS FACTS FACTS

Salmon are anadromous. They are born in fresh water, migrate to the
ocean, then return to fresh water to reproduce. They even return to
the exact spot where they were born. Usually at least 90% of the
fish spawning in a stream were born there.

Clam Sauce with Linguine

1 package linguine pasta
1 dl (1/2 cup) butter
3 cloves garlic, chopped
450 g (1 lb) fresh mushrooms, sliced
2 cans clams with juice, chopped
1 dl (1/2 cup) fresh parsley, chopped
1 tsp salt
1/2 tsp ground white pepper
1/2 dl (1/4 cup) grated Parmesan cheese

Cook pasta for 8 to 10 minutes or until al dente.
Sauté garlic and mushrooms in butter until golden brown.
Stir in clams with juice, parsley, salt and white pepper.
Cook over medium heat until hot.
Toss with pasta until evenly coated.
Serve with Parmesan cheese.

FACTS FACTS FACTS

Linguine means "little tongues" in Italian.

Creamy Crab Pasta

1 package bow tie pasta
1 can condensed cream of celery soup
3 dl (10 3/4 oz) milk
1 package cream cheese
350 g (3/4 lb) imitation crabmeat, flaked
1 bunch green onions, sliced
2 1/2 dl (1 cup) frozen green peas

Cook pasta 12 minutes, until al dente. In a saucepan over medium heat, blend the cream of celery soup, milk, and cream cheese. Mix in the imitation crabmeat and green onions. In a bowl, toss together the pasta, crabmeat mixture, and frozen green peas.

FACTS FACTS FACTS

Crab lice, Phthirus pubis, is commonly called "crabs" due to their resemblance to the crab. Crab lice are easily killed with a 1% permethrin or pyrethrin lice shampoo, but the pubic hair must be combed with a fine-toothed comb after treatment to remove the nits.

Penne with Shrimp

1 package penne pasta
2 tbsp olive oil
1/2 dl (1/4 cup) red onion, chopped
1 tbsp garlic, chopped
1/2 dl (1/4 cup) white wine
2 cans diced tomatoes
450 g (1 lb) shrimp, peeled and deveined
2 1/2 dl (1 cup) grated Parmesan cheese

Cook pasta for 8 to 10 minutes or until al dente.
Heat oil in a skillet over medium heat. Stir in onion and garlic,
and cook until tender. Mix in wine and tomatoes, and continue
cooking 10 minutes. Mix shrimp into the skillet, and cook
5 minutes. Toss with pasta and top with Parmesan cheese to serve.

QUOTES QUOTES QUOTES

"-Hey George, the ocean called, they're running out of shrimp."

-Seinfeld

Quick
Clam Spaghetti

1 package spaghetti
2 tbspolive oil
2 cloves garlic, chopped
2 cans clams with juice, chopped
1 dl (1/2 cup) fresh parsley, chopped
1 dl (1/2 cup) grated Parmesan cheese
Fresh parsley for garnish

Cook spaghetti for 8 to 10 minutes, until al dente.
In a skillet, sauté the garlic one minute, until tender. Mix in the
clams and juice. Cook until liquid is reduced to about 1 dl (1/2
cup). In a large bowl, toss the spaghetti with the sautéed clams,
chopped parsley, and Parmesan cheese. Garnish with parsley to
serve.

TRIVIA TRIVIA TRIVIA

The Giant Clam (Tridacna gigas) can weigh more than 400
pounds and measure as much as 1.5 meters across.

Shrimp Avocado Pasta Salad

1 package uncooked penne pasta
100 g (1/4 lb) bacon
450 g (1 lb) cooked shrimp, peeled and deveined
2 avocados, peeled and diced
2 1/2 dl (1 cup) Cheddar cheese, shredded
2 1/2 dl (1 cup) mayonnaise
1/2 dl (1/4 cup) lemon juice
2 tomatoes, diced
1 tsp crushed red pepper
9 1/2 dl (4 cups) lettuce, shredded

Cook pasta for 8 to 10 minutes, until al dente. Rinse under cold running water to cool. Cook bacon in a skillet until evenly brown. Drain and crumble. In a large bowl, gently toss together the pasta, bacon, shrimp, avocados, Cheddar cheese, mayonnaise, lemon juice, tomatoes, and red pepper. Serve over lettuce.

QUOTES QUOTES QUOTES

"-Anyway, like I was sayin', shrimp is the fruit of the sea. You can barbecue it, boil it, broil it, bake it, sauté it. Dey's uh, shrimp-kabobs, shrimp Creole, shrimp gumbo. Pan fried, deep fried, stir-fried. There's pineapple shrimp, lemon shrimp, coconut shrimp, pepper shrimp, shrimp soup, shrimp stew, shrimp salad, shrimp and potatoes, shrimp burger, shrimp sandwich. That- that's about it. "

-Forrest Gump

Tuna and Noodles

1 package egg noodles
350 g (3/4 lb) prepared cheese product
200 g (1 8 ounce package) Cheddar cheese
1 package frozen vegetables blend, thawed
1 can tuna, flaked
1/4 tsp pepper

Cook noodles until done. Do not drain. Add cheese, vegetables, tuna and pepper. Stir until melted. Serve with whole wheat rolls and a tossed salad.

FACTS FACTS FACTS

Dolphins are aquatic mammals and the name comes from Ancient Greek meaning "with a womb". The military has employed dolphins for finding mines and rescuing lost or trapped persons. During the Vietnam War dolphins were even being trained to kill Vietnamese Skin Divers.

Spicy Red Lentil Soup
(VEGGIE)

1 tsp olive oil
3 1/2 dl (1 1/2 cups) red onion, chopped
Salt and pepper to taste
800 g (28 oz) diced tomatoes, canned
3 1/2 dl (1 1/2 cups) spinach, chopped
5 dl (2 cups) uncooked red lentils
5 dl (2 cups) water
2 tsp dried basil
1 1/2 tsp ground cardamom
1 tsp ground cumin
1/2 tsp ground cayenne pepper
1/2 tsp curry powder

Cook the onion in oil until golden brown. Season with salt and pepper. Mix in tomatoes, spinach, and lentils, and pour in water. Season with basil, cardamom, cumin, cayenne pepper, and curry powder. Bring to a boil, and let simmer for 25 minutes, stirring occasionally, until lentils are tender. Use a blender and blend until smooth before serving.

TRIVIA TRIVIA TRIVIA

The Spice Girls are the biggest-selling girl group of all time, selling in excess of forty-five million albums with only three LPs released. They have also sold in excess of thirty million singles, the most ever for a female group.

Macaroni Salad
(VEGGIE)

5 dl (2 cups) macaroni
1 small onion, chopped
1 green bell pepper, chopped
1 carrot, grated
1/2 dl (1/4 cup) mayonnaise
1/2 dl (1/4 cup) ranch-style salad dressing

Cook pasta for 8 to 10 minutes or until al dente.
Rinse with cold water and place in large bowl.
Add onion, pepper and carrot.
Toss with mayonnaise and ranch-style dressing.

TRIVIA TRIVIA TRIVIA

Macaroni is a corruption of the Italian word maccherone and its plural maccheroni. Calabrians usually refer to pastas as maccheroni, and the Calabrian girls used to have to be skilled at making 15 types of pasta in order to be considered for marriage, maccheroni being a requirement.

Olive Oil, Tomato, and Basil Pasta
(VEGGIE)

1 package farfalle pasta
2 tomatoes, diced
1 dl (1/2 cup) olive oil
2 cloves garlic, minced
1 dl (1/2 cup) fresh basil leaves, minced
Salt and pepper to taste

Cook pasta for 8 to 10 minutes or until al dente.
In a large bowl, gently toss the cooked pasta, tomatoes, olive oil, garlic, and basil. Season with salt and pepper.

TRIVIA TRIVIA TRIVIA

If YOU have questions about olive oil, contact:
International Olive Oil Council
Address: Príncipe de Vergara 154
28002, Madrid. Spain
Tel: 34 915 903 638
Fax: 34 915 631 263
E-mail:iooc@internationaloliveoil.org

Tofu Curry Salad
(VEGGIE)

1 dl (1/2 cup) white rice
5 dl (2 cups) extra-firm tofu, drained and cubed
2 1/2 dl (1 cup) yogurt
2 tbsp lime juice
1 tbsp curry powder
2 1/2 dl (1 cup) grapes, halved
1 tbsp dried cranberries
1 dl (1/2 cup) celery, diced
3 tbsp green onions, diced
1/2 dl (1/4 cup) walnuts
Salt and pepper to taste

Cook rice for 20 minutes and set aside.
Boil water and cook cubed tofu for 3 minutes. Drain and set aside
to cool. In a bowl, blend yogurt with lime juice and curry powder.
In a large mixing bowl, toss halved grapes, cranberries, celery,
green onions, walnuts, rice, and tofu. Drizzle with curry dressing,
and toss until well coated.
Season with salt and pepper before serving.

QUOTES QUOTES QUOTES

"-I realize that when I met you at the turkey curry buffet,
I was unforgivably rude, and wearing a reindeer jumper."

-Bridget Jones's Diary

Black Beans and Rice
(VEGGIE)

2 1/2 dl (1 cup) uncooked white rice
2 tbsp vegetable oil
1 package frozen green bell peppers and onions
1 can black beans, undrained
1 can enchilada sauce

Cook rice for 20 minutes.
Meanwhile, heat oil in a large skillet and sauté peppers
and onions until tender. Stir in beans and enchilada sauce,
let simmer for 15 minutes.
Serve over cooked rice.

FACTS FACTS FACTS

In 1889, Justice Joseph Philo Bradley of the United States Supreme Court
ruled, in Robertson v. Salomon (130 U. S. 412), that a bean is a vegetable
and not a seed. In his decision, Bradley stated that:

"-We do not see why they should be classified as seeds, any more
than walnuts should be so classified. Both are seeds, in the language of
botany or natural history, but not in commerce nor in common parlance.
Beyond the common knowledge which we have on this subject, very little
evidence is necessary, or can be produced."

And that's that.

Lima Bean Pasta
(VEGGIE)

1 package pasta
1/2 dl (1/4 cup) olive oil
1 can lima beans, drained
2 cloves garlic, crushed
1 tsp dried tarragon
1/8 tsp salt
1 dl (1/2 cup) grated Parmesan cheese

Cook pasta for 8 to 10 minutes, until al dente.
Heat the olive oil in a skillet and fry the lima beans.
Season with garlic, tarragon, and salt. Cook and stir until heated through. Toss with cooked pasta and top with Parmesan cheese to serve.

TRIVIA TRIVIA TRIVIA

Lima is the capital and largest city in Peru.
Founded by Spanish conquistador Francisco Pizarro, Lima is also known as the City of Kings. For more than three centuries, Lima was the most important city and the greatest metropolis in South America.

Pasta Siciliano
(VEGGIE)

1 package farfalle pasta
1/2 dl (1/4 cup) olive oil
3 cloves garlic, chopped
1 tsp crushed red pepper flakes
2 tbsp lemon juice
1 dl (1/2 cup) pine nuts
1 small can black olives, sliced
1 dl (1/2 cup) sun-dried tomatoes, chopped
2 1/2 dl (1 cup) feta cheese, crumbled
Salt and pepper to taste

Cook pasta for 8 to 10 minutes, until al dente.
Heat the oil in a large skillet and cook the garlic until lightly browned. Mix in red pepper and lemon juice. Stir in the pine nuts, olives, and sun-dried tomatoes. Toss in the cooked pasta and feta cheese. Season with salt and pepper.

QUOTES QUOTES QUOTES

"-In Sicily, women are more dangerous than shotguns."

-The Godfather

Oriental Chicken Noodle Soup

7 dl (3 cups) water
1 package chicken flavored ramen noodles
5 dl (2 cups) cooked chicken breast, chopped
2 leaves bok choy, sliced
1 carrot, sliced
1 tsp sesame oil

Bring water to boil. Break up block of noodles and stir into pot, reserving seasoning packet. Stir in chicken, bok choy and carrot. Bring to a boil again, and let simmer for 3 minutes.
Stir in seasoning packet and sesame oil.

QUOTES QUOTES QUOTES

"-A good fight should be like a small play but played seriously. When the opponent expands, I contract. When he contracts, I expand. And when the opportunity presents itself, I do not hit. It hits all by itself. "

-Enter the Dragon

Beef Enchiladas

450 g (1 lb) lean ground beef
1 small onion, chopped
1 package dry enchilada sauce mix
10 flour tortillas
5 dl (2 cups) Cheddar cheese, shredded
1 small can black olives, sliced

Preheat oven to 350 degrees F (175 degrees C).
Cook the ground beef and onion in a skillet, until beef is evenly browned. Prepare the enchilada sauce according to package directions. Pour 1/2 dl (1/4 cup) of the sauce into the bottom of a 23x33 cm (9x13 inch) baking dish. On each flour tortilla, place an equal portion of the ground beef mixture and about 3 dl (1 cup) of Cheddar cheese. Tightly roll the tortillas and place seam side down in the baking dish. Pour the remaining sauce over the top of the enchiladas
and sprinkle with the remaining cheese and olives. Bake in a preheated oven for 20 minutes, until cheese is thoroughly melted. Serve with a green salad or beans and rice.

FACTS FACTS FACTS

The best and most expensive beef in the world is Kobe Beef, from Japan.
The cows that produce Kobe Beef are massaged daily and fed beer
to increase the quality of the meat. Kobe Beef costs over $100
per pound in Japan.

Hearty Meat Sauce

200 g (1/2 lb) ground beef
2 jars spaghetti sauce
1 yellow pepper, diced
1 red bell pepper, diced
1 can peeled and diced tomatoes, drained
6 fresh mushrooms, chopped

Brown the ground beef in a skillet until no pink shows.
In a pot, combine browned beef and spaghetti sauce over medium heat for 5 or 10 minutes. Add yellow peppers, red peppers, canned tomatoes and mushrooms. Lower heat and let simmer, covered, for 30 minutes.

FUN FUN FUN

In 1977, the state of New York hired advertising agency Well, Rich and Green to develop a marketing campaign for New York City. Milton Glaser, a productive commercial artist, created the "I (heart) NY" design. Glaser expected the campaign to last only a couple months and did the work pro bono.

Shrimp and Rice

7 dl (3 cups) hot cooked rice
1 can sweet corn
1/2 dl (1/4 cup) sun-dried tomatoes, chopped
2 1/2 dl (1 cup) Italian cheese, shredded
1/2 dl (1/4 cup) fresh basil leaves, chopped
1/2 tsp salt
450 g (1 lb) shrimp, peeled and deveined

In a large bowl, combine rice, corn, sun-dried tomatoes, cheese, basil and salt. Brush shrimp with reserved oil from tomatoes. Broil in oven 10 to 13 cm (4 to 5 inches) from heat for 4 minutes. Top rice with shrimp and serve.

FACTS FACTS FACTS

A shrimp's heart is in its head.

Salmon Burgers

1 can salmon, drained
8 saltines
1/2 dl (1/4 cup) red pepper, diced
3 tbsp mayonnaise
1 tbsp lemon juice
4 drops Tabasco sauce
4 lettuce leaves
1 tomato, sliced
4 hamburger buns

In a medium-sized bowl, remove skin from fish and flake with a fork. Crush the crackers and add to the bowl. Add red pepper, mayonnaise, lemon juice and Tabasco. Mix well. Shape into 4 patties. Cook salmon cakes in a skillet, turning once, until lightly browned on each side. Serve on buns topped with lettuce and tomato.

QUOTES QUOTES QUOTES

"-And you know what they call a Quarter Pounder with Cheese in Paris?
-They don't call it a Quarter Pounder with cheese?
-No man, they got the metric system. They wouldn't know what the fuck a Quarter Pounder is.
-Then what do they call it?
-They call it a Royale with cheese.
-A Royale with cheese. What do they call a Big Mac?
-Well, a Big Mac's a Big Mac, but they call it le Big-Mac."

-Pulp Fiction

Mexican Oven Baked Fish

3 1/2 dl (1 1/2 lb) cod fillets
2 1/2 dl (1 cup) salsa
2 1/2 dl (1 cup) sharp Cheddar cheese, shredded
1 dl (1/2 cup) corn chips, crushed
1 avocado, sliced
1/2 dl (1/4 cup) sour cream

Preheat oven to 400 degrees F (205 degrees C).
Rinse fish fillets under cold water and pat dry with paper towels.
Lay fillets side-by-side in a greased baking dish. Pour the salsa
over the top and sprinkle evenly with the shredded cheese. Top
with the crushed corn chips. Bake in oven for 15 minutes or until
fish flakes with a fork. Serve topped with sliced avocado and
sour cream.

FACTS FACTS FACTS

The Mexi part of Mexico is from Mexitli, the war god, whose name
was derived from metztli (the moon) and xictli (navel) and thus
meant "navel of the moon". So, Mexico is the home of
the people of Mexitli.

Beef and Mushroom Risotto

450 g (1 lb) lean ground beef
1 package (150 g / 5 1/2 ounces) risotto mix with garden vegetables
3 1/2 dl (1 1/2 cup) sliced mushrooms
2 1/2 dl (1 cup) chopped red bell pepper
2 cloves garlic crushed
1/2 tsp salt
1/4 tsp pepper
2 tbsp grated parmesan cheese
1 tbsp chopped fresh Basil

Prepare risotto mix according to package directions.
Meanwhile, in a large nonstick skillet, brown ground beef,
mushrooms, bell pepper and garlic over medium heat 8 - 10
minutes or until beef is no longer pink, breaking beef up into small
crumbles. Pour off drippings. Season with salt and pepper.
Stir risotto into beef mixture. Sprinkle with cheese and basil.

TRIVIA TRIVIA TRIVIA

Psilocybin, an extract of certain psychedelic mushrooms, is being
studied for its ability to help people suffering from mental disease,
such as Obsessive-compulsive disorder. Minute amounts have also
been reported to stop migraine headaches.

Spaghetti 'n' Meatballs

1 package spaghetti
1 jar spaghetti sauce
1 batch pre-cooked meatballs
Parmesan cheese, grated

Cook spaghetti according to package directions.
Meanwhile, in a saucepan, combine spaghetti sauce and
meatballs, cover and simmer for 15-20 minutes or until the
meatballs are heated through. Serve over spaghetti,
top with Parmesan cheese.

FUN FUN FUN

In the Disney film Lady and the Tramp, the film's opening sequence, in
which Darling unwraps a hat box on Christmas morning and finds Lady
inside, is based upon an actual incident in Walt Disney's life. After he'd
forgotten a dinner date with his wife, he made it up to her by offering
her the puppy-in-the-hat-box surprise and was immediately forgiven.

Greek Lasagna
(VEGGIE)

800 g (28 oz) tomato and basil pasta sauce, canned
9 lasagna noodles, uncooked
1 package fresh baby spinach
1 dl (1/2 cup) red onion, chopped
1 dl (1/2 cup) red bell pepper, chopped
2 1/2 dl (1 cup) olives, sliced
800 g (28 oz) diced, peeled tomatoes, canned
16 basil leaves
2 1/2 dl (1 cup) mozzarella cheese, shredded
5 dl (2 cups) feta cheese, crumbled

Microwave onion and pepper together on high power 1 to 2 minutes until softened. Spoon 2 1/2 dl (1 cup) pasta sauce over bottom of a rectangular baking dish. Top with 3 uncooked lasagna noodles. Spread evenly with 1/2 of package of spinach, then sprinkle evenly with all of onion-red pepper mixture, 1/2 of olive pieces, 1/2 of drained tomato pieces, 8 basil leaves, 1 dl (1/2 cup) shredded mozzarella and 2 1/2 dl (1 cup) crumbled feta. Add 1/2 of remaining sauce, spreading evenly. Add another layer of 3 noodles, remaining spinach leaves, remaining olive pieces, tomato pieces, basil leaves and crumbled feta. Add remaining 3 noodles and sauce.
Cover tightly with foil. Bake in preheated 375° oven for 50 to 55 minutes. Remove cover, top with 1 1/2 dl (1/2 cup) mozzarella cheese and bake 5 to 10 minutes longer. Let stand 10 to 15 minutes before serving.

QUOTES QUOTES QUOTES

"-There are two kinds of people - Greeks, and everyone else who wish they was Greek."

-My Big Fat Greek Wedding

Scrambled eggs

2 large eggs
1 tbsp milk or cream
Pinch of salt
Pinch of black pepper
1 tsp butter

Use a fork and beat the eggs with milk, salt and pepper in a small bowl. Melt butter and pour the egg mixture into a skillet. Let cook for 1-2 minutes, using a spatula to mix the eggs until they are no longer runny.

FACTS FACTS FACTS

The working title for the tune "Yesterday", by The Beatles was "Scrambled Eggs", before Paul McCartney came up with the current lyrics.

Breakfast Burrito

2 large eggs
1 tbsp milk
Pinch of salt
Pinch of black pepper
1 tsp butter
1 large flour tortilla
1/2 dl (1/4 cup) shredded cheddar or jack cheese
1 tbsp salsa
1/4 avocado, sliced

Use a fork and beat the eggs with milk, salt and pepper in a small bowl. Melt butter and pour the egg mixture into a skillet.
Let it cook for 1-2 minutes, using a spatula to mix the eggs until they are no longer runny.
Heat a larger skillet and place the tortilla in it. Top with cheese and heat until the cheese starts to melt.
Put the tortilla on a plate and pour the cooked eggs in the center.
Top with salsa, avocado and a pinch of salt.
Roll up the burrito and serve.

FACTS FACTS FACTS

In Korea, breakfast has not existed as a distinct concept. Food eaten in the morning does not differ substantially from the other meals of the day. Fermented vegetables and rice, for example, are staples of the morning meal.

Turkey Burgers with Pesto

450 g (1 lb) ground turkey
1/2 dl (1/4 cup) pesto
1/2 tsp salt
Pinch of black pepper
2 tsp vegetable oil
4 hamburger buns
1/2 dl (1/4 cup) mayonnaise
4 lettuce leaves
1 tomato, sliced
1 red onion, thinly sliced

Mix turkey, pesto, salt and black pepper in a large bowl. With your hands, shape 11 1/2 cm (4 1/2-inch) thick patties and place the burgers in a heated and oiled skillet. Cook for 6 to 8 minutes, until bottom is golden. Flip and cook the other side. Spread the buns with mayo and top the burgers with lettuce, tomato and red onion.

QUOTES QUOTES QUOTES

"-You can't have Thanksgiving without turkey. That's like Fourth of July without apple pie, or Friday with no two pizzas."

-Friends

Hamburgers

450 g (1 lb) ground beef
1 large egg
1 garlic clove, minced
1 tbsp Worcestershire sauce
1/2 tsp salt
Pinch of black pepper
4 cheese slices
4 hamburger buns
Ketchup
Mustard
4 lettuce leaves
1 tomato, sliced
1 red onion, sliced

Mix together ground beef, egg, garlic, Worcestershire sauce, salt and pepper in a large bowl. Shape the mixture into 11 cm (4 1/4-inch) thick patties and place the burgers in a heated skillet. Cook until the bottom is brown and the sides no longer red. Flip over and cook the other side. Lay cheese slices over burgers and cook
until melted. Serve the hamburgers on buns with ketchup, mustard, lettuce, tomato and red onion.

TRIVIA TRIVIA TRIVIA

The world's most expensive burger used to be at the Old Homestead Steakhouse, in New York. They offered a $41 Kobe beef burger, but soon after the release, DB Bistro Moderne answered with a $50 burger, made with sirloin steak, a filling of boned short ribs braised in red wine, foie gras, and preserved black truffles. It remains to be seen if Old Homestead Steakhouse will top this price.

Fettucine Alfredo

200 g (8 oz) fettucine
Pinch of salt
2 tbsp butter
1 dl (1/2 cup) whipping cream
1 dl (1/2 cup) grated parmesan cheese
Pinch of black pepper

Bring a large saucepan filled with water to boil. Add a pinch of salt. Add the fettucine and cook according to package. Drain. Melt the butter in the saucepan and return the pasta to it. Add cream and parmesan cheese stirring constantly. Add a pinch of salt and pepper before serving.

FACTS FACTS FACTS

Alfredo sauce was invented in Rome in 1914 by restaurant owner Alfredo di Lello. His restaurant attracted many celebrities, two of which were Mary Pickford and Douglas Fairbanks. On their return to the United States, they asked for the same recipe, and thus introduced it to the New World. Since then Alfredo has been far more popular in the United States than in Italy, where it is mostly served to American tourists.

Asian Peanut Noodles

1 package udon or soba noodles
1 dl (1/2 cup) creamy peanut butter
1 garlic clove, minced
2 tbsp soy sauce
1/2 dl (1/4 tsp) sugar
1/2 dl (1/4 tsp) cayenne
1 lime
1 dl (1/2 cup) hot water
1 carrot, peeled and shredded
2 green onions, chopped

Bring a large saucepan filled with water to boil. Add the noodles and cook until tender, 8 to 10 minutes. Place peanut butter, garlic, soy sauce, sugar and cayenne in a bowl. Squeeze the lime over it. Add 1 dl (1/2 cup) hot water and stir to combine. Drain noodles and transfer to bowl, along with the carrot and onions.

FACTS FACTS FACTS

The Tanganyika Groundnut Scheme was a plan to cultivate tracts of what is now Tanzania with peanuts. The project was a brainchild of the British Labour government of Clement Attlee. It was abandoned at considerable cost to the taxpayers after it was discovered that peanuts will not grow in Tanganyika.

Rice and Beans

4 slices bacon, diced
1 onion, diced
1 stalk celery, diced
2 garlic cloves, minced
1 small hot chile, seeded and minced
2 cans black beans, drained
1 dl (1/2 cup) water
Pinch of salt
Pinch of black pepper
Tomato salsa
Sour cream

Cook the rice, following package directions. Fry the bacon in a saucepan until crispy. Remove bacon from heat, and add onion and celery to the saucepan. Sauté for a couple of minutes. Add garlic and chile and sauté for another minute. Add black beans and water, and bring to boil. Let it simmer for 10 minutes. Add the bacon and salt and pepper. Serve with rice, tomato salsa and sour cream.

FUN FUN FUN

An anatomically-correct computer model of Kevin Bacon's entire body was made for the movie Hollow Man. This model was later donated to scientists.

Parmesan Couscous

2 1/2 dl (1 cup) water
2 1/2 dl (1 cup) instant couscous
1 dl (1/2 cup) frozen peas
1 tbsp butter
1 dl (1/3 cup) grated parmesan cheese
Pinch of salt
Pinch of black pepper

Heat water on a stove or in a microwave. Pour it over the couscous in a medium bowl and set aside. Melt the butter and thaw peas in the microwave. Add peas, butter and parmesan cheese to the couscous and fluff it with a fork. Season with salt and pepper.

TRIVIA TRIVIA TRIVIA

Peas pudding hot,
Peas pudding cold,
Peas pudding in the pot,
Nine days old

Some like it hot,
Some like it cold,
Some like it in the pot
Nine days old

Asian Dumpling Soup

1 container chicken or vegetable broth
8 to 12 frozen meat or vegetable dumplings
2 tsp soy sauce
1 green onion, chopped
Pinch of red pepper

Heat the broth in a large saucepan. Add the dumplings and bring to boil. Let simmer for about 5 minutes. Add soy sauce. Serve in bowls and top with the green onion and red pepper.

QUOTES QUOTES QUOTES

"-You know that feeling when the huge dump you just took shoots back up inside your ass?"

-South Park

Corn on the Cob

4 large ears of fresh corn
Butter
Pinch of salt

Bring 2 quarts of water to boil. Pull the husks off of the ears of corn and remove the silk. Cook for 6 to 8 minutes, or until the kernels are tender. Serve with butter and salt.

FACTS FACTS FACTS

Maize is called corn in the United States, and prior to harvest it's popular to build "corn mazes" in many farming communities. The first modern corn maze was designed by Adrian Fisher, who is in the Guinness Book of World Records for several of his maze designs.

Mashed Potatoes

4 medium baking potatoes
2 tbsp butter
1/2 to 1 dl (1/4 to 1/2 cup) milk
1/4 tsp salt
Pinch of black pepper

Peel the potatoes and cut them into 2 1/2 cm (1-inch) pieces.
Place in saucepan, cover with water and bring to boil.
Let simmer until potatoes are tender. Drain and mash with a fork.
Add butter and mash to combine. Add milk and stir. Season with
salt and pepper.

QUOTES QUOTES QUOTES

"-I know, I'll marry Lynn. Become a citizen, vote,
then drop her like a hot potato."

-ALF

Noodle Salad

1 package soba or udon noodles
2 green onions, thinly sliced
1 1/2 tsp minced fresh ginger
1 garlic clove, minced
2 tbsp rice vinegar
2 tbsp soy sauce
1 tbsp vegetable oil
1/2 dl (1/4 cup) frozen peas
1 tbsp sesame seeds

Bring water to boil in a big saucepan. Add noodles and cook according to package. Place the onion, ginger, garlic, vinegar, soy sauce, vegetable oil and peas in a large bowl.
Drain noodles and add to bowl. Mix well.
Sprinkle sesame seeds on top before serving.

FACTS FACTS FACTS

By federal law, a noodle must contain 5.5 percent egg solids to be called a noodle. So without egg, a noodle really isn't a noodle.

Tomato Mozzarella Salad with Basil

4 slices tomato
4 leaves fresh basil
4 slices mozzarella
Pinch of black pepper

Place tomatoes on a plate. Top with basil leaves and mozzarella and season with black pepper.

QUOTES QUOTES QUOTES

"-Vincent, do you still want to hear my Fox Force Five joke?
-Sure, but I think I'm still a little too petrified to laugh…
-No, you won't laugh, 'cus it's not funny.
But if you still wanna hear it, I'll tell it.
-I can't wait.
-Three tomatoes are walking down the street- a poppa tomato, a momma tomato, and a little baby tomato. Baby tomato starts lagging behind. Poppa tomato gets angry, goes over to the baby tomato, and smooshes him… and says, ketchup."

-Pulp Fiction

Veggie Chili

Vegetable oil
1 yellow onion, diced
2 green peppers, diced
2 cans stewed whole tomatoes
2 cans black beans
1 can corn
1 can kidney beans
1/2 tbsp chili powder
1 tsp cayenne
1/2 tsp cinnamon
Salt and pepper to taste
2 tomatoes, diced
5 dl (2 cups) Cheddar cheese

Sauté the onions and peppers in vegetable oil in a large pot. Add all the canned ingredients as well as the chili powder, cayenne and cinnamon. Bring to boil and let it simmer for 30 minutes. Season with salt and pepper. Top each bowl with diced tomatoes and cheddar cheese before serving.

TRIVIA TRIVIA TRIVIA

Chili is a town located in Monroe County, New York, established in 1822. The town has a total population of about 30,000. The name Chili was chosen due to sympathy for the revolution for independence in Chile.

Sesame Noodles

1 package soba or udon noodles
4 tbsp peanut buter
2 tsp sesame oil
1/2 tsp vinegar
1 tbsp scallions, chopped

Cook the noodles and drain. Cook peanut butter and sesame oil in the microwave for 30 seconds, until it starts to melt. Mix it with the noodles and add scallions.

QUOTES QUOTES QUOTES

"-Today, we bring you greatest play in English language: Hamlet, by William Shakespeare. It no get classier than this."

-Sesame Street

Pasta with Shrimp and Feta

2 tsp olive oil
2 cloves garlic, minced
2 1/2 dl (1 cup) onion, chopped
5 dl (2 cups) tomato sauce
1 tomato, chopped
Oregano
Basil
1 dl (1/2 cup) white wine
450 g (1 lb) raw shrimp, shelled and deveined
200 g (1/2 of a 16-oz pack) spaghetti, cooked
1 dl (1/2 cup) feta cheese

Sauté garlic and onion in olive oil, in a large skillet. Add tomato sauce and tomatoed and cook for a couple of minutes. Add the wine and bring to boil. Then add the shrimp and cook until pink. Spoon sauce over the newly cooked pasta and crumble feta cheese on top before serving.

TRIVIA TRIVIA TRIVIA

To cook one billion pounds of pasta, you would need 2,021,452,000 gallons of water - enough to fill nearly 75,000 Olympic-size swimming pools.

Ramen Noodle Stir-Fry

1 package ramen noodles
1 tsp olive oil
1/2 dl (1/4 cup) green pepper, chopped
1/2 dl (1/4 cup) red pepper, chopped
1/2 dl (1/4 cup) onion, chopped
1 clove garlic, minced
1 tsp hot sauce
Oregano
Cayenne

Boil noodles until tender. Saute peppers, onion and garlic in the oil. Add the hot sauce, oregano and cayenne, and let simmer for 5 minutes. Add noodles and cook for another 1 minute. Serve.

FUN FUN FUN

The Shin-Yokohama Ramen Museum in Japan, is the world's first food Ramen museum, and it opened on March 3, 1994. The museum is devoted to the Japanese ramen noodle soup and features a large recreation of Tokyo in the year 1958, the year instant noodles was invented.

Chicken Pesto Pasta

5 dl (2 cups) fresh basil leaves
1 dl (1/3 cup) parmesan cheese, grated
3 cloves garlic, minced
1/2 tsp salt
1/2 tsp pepper
1 dl (1/2 cup) olive oil
200 g (1/2 of a 16-ounce box) penne pasta
3 chicken breasts, cut into strips

Combine basil, parmesan, garlic, salt and pepper in a blender. Add the olive oil and blend until smooth. Cook the pasta until tender. Drain. Sauté the chicken in a skillet until cooked though. Pour pesto over pasta and mix in chicken. Serve.

FACTS FACTS FACTS

The first American pasta factory was opened in Brooklyn, New York, in 1848, by a Frenchman named Antoine Zerega. Mr. Zerega managed the entire operation with just one horse in his basement to power the machinery. To dry his spaghetti, he placed strands of the pasta on the roof to dry in the sunshine.

Mexican Lasagna

1 onion, chopped
1/2 green pepper, chopped
2 tsp olive oil
3 cloves garlic, minced
550 g (1 1/4 lb) ground beef
2 tbsp jalapeno, chopped
5 dl (2 cups) tomato sauce
3 1/2 dl (1 1/2 cups) beef broth
1 tbsp flour
Pinch of salt
6 small tortillas, cut into three strips each
3 tbsp cilantro, chopped
5 dl (2 cups) cheddar cheese, shredded

Heat oven to 350 degrees F (180 degrees C).
Sauté onion and green pepper in oil. Add garlic and cook
another 2 minutes. Add beef and cook until brown.
Stir in jalapeno, tomato sauce and half of the beef broth.
Let simmer. Mix the flour with the remaining beef broth and add
to pot. Let it simmer until the sauce thickens. Remove from the
heat and add cilantro. Fill a casserole dish with sauce, cheese
and tortillas in alternating layers. End with a cheese layer and
bake for 15 minutes.

QUOTES QUOTES QUOTES

"-Once again, my life has been saved by the miracle of lasagna."

-Garfield

Sloppy Joe's

700 g (1 1/2 lb) ground beef
1/2 onion, chopped
1 clove garlic, minced
1 dl (1/2 cup) ketchup
1/2 dl (1/4 cup) tomato sauce
1 tbsp red wine vinegar
2 tbsp Worcestershire sauce
2 tsp hot sauce
Salt and pepper
4 hamburger buns

Brown the beef, onion and garlic in a skillet. Add ketchup, crushed tomatoes, vinegar, Worcestershire sauce, hot sauce, and salt and pepper. Let simmer for 5 minutes. Toast the buns and put a big portion of the beef mixture over each before serving.

FACTS FACTS FACTS

Sloppy Joe's Bar in Key West, Florida, opened in 1933 and was originally named "The Blind Pig". One day a man walked in and said to the owner (Josie Russel), "-Joe, you sure do run a sloppy place. You should call this place Sloppy Joe's."
That man was no other than Ernest Hemingway.

Read these great Hemingway books: The Old Man and the Sea, For Whom the Bells Tolls, Sun Also Rises, A Farewell to Arms.

Sloppy Joe's Annual Papa Look-Alike Contest.
In mid-July each year, Sloppy Joe's, in Key West, Florida, is thronged with cheerful bearded men competing for the title of Hemingway Look-A-Like, while Hemingway family members judge their worthiness and hundreds of spectators cheer on their favorites. Be there or be square.

Spaghetti Carbonara

1 package spaghetti
450 g (1 lb) bacon, chopped
4 eggs, beaten
2 1/2 (1 cup) Parmesan cheese, grated
1/2 (1/4 cup) olive oil
1 clove garlic

Cook pasta for 8 to 10 minutes until al dente.
Meanwhile, cook bacon with garlic, until evenly brown. Crumble and set aside. Scramble eggs in the bacon drippings.
Place spaghetti in a large bowl. Pour in olive oil, and mix well. Stir in bacon, eggs, and Parmesan cheese. Serve immediately.

FACTS FACTS FACTS

Spaghetti Carbonara dates back to the Roman period. The name is derived from the Italian word for charcoal. Some say the pasta was first made as a hearty dish for Italian charcoal miners.

Truck Driver Breakfast

Fried bacon
Fried sausage
Scrambled eggs
Ketchup
Pancakes with Maple syrup
Toast with butter
Grits
Coffee
Orange Juice

QUOTES QUOTES QUOTES

"-I drive trucks, break arms, and arm wrestle.
It's what I love to do, it's what I do best."

"-My whole body is an engine.
This is a fireplug ... and I'm gonna light him up."

-Over the Top

Hungover Pizza

1 phone
1 phone number to a pizza place with delivery service.

When hunger battles headache about who hurts the most, then it's time to order a hungover pizza. Pick up the phone with which ever hand is closest, and collect all the power left in your alcohol-ridden brain to dial the number to your local pizzeria. Mumble something about your choice of pizza and make them cut it up in easy-to-handle slices for you. Once the pizza has arrived, throw yourself on the sofa, put a 80s comedy in the player and dig in. God knows you've deserved it after all this work!

QUOTES QUOTES QUOTES

"-Old Mc Bundy had a farm, B-U-N-D-Y. And on this farm there was no wife, B-U-N-D-Y. With-a no wife here and a-no kids there. A hooker coming over on Friday nights. With big luscious hooters, a pizza, and a beer there. Old Mc Bundy had a farm, B-U-N-D-Y."

-Married… with Children

Brunch

Classic Brunch:
scrambled eggs, bacon, fresh fruit, green salad,
newly baked muffins, juice and coffee.

New York Style Brunch:
smoked salmon, cream cheese, onion rings and capers on a
bagel, and a New York Times.

QUOTES QUOTES QUOTES

"-It's not quite breakfast, it's not quite lunch, but it comes
with a slice of cantaloupe at the end."

-The Simpsons

Swedish Meatballs

3 1/2 dl (1 1/2 cups) soft bread crumbs (about 3 slices bread crumbled)
1/2 dl (1/4 cup) finely chopped onion
1 1/2 tsp salt
1/4 tsp pepper
1/4 tsp nutmeg
1 1/2 dl (3/4 cup) milk
900 g (2 lb) ground beef
2 tbsp butter
2 tbsp vegetable oil
2 tbsp flour
1 can condensed beef broth
2 1/2 dl (1 cup) light cream

Combine bread crumbs, onion, salt, pepper, nutmeg and 1 1/2 dl (3/4 cup) milk in a large mixing bowl. Let milk soak into crumbs for a few minutes. Gently stir in ground beef until well blended and form into balls about 1 to 3 1/2 cm (1 1/2 inches) in diameter. Brown meatballs in butter and oil in a large skillet. Remove with a slotted spoon to a 2 1/2-quart baking dish. Stir flour into drippings. Cook, stirring constantly, until bubbly. Stir in beef broth and cream. Continue cooking, stirring constantly, until sauce thickens and boils for a minute. Pour over meatballs in baking dish.
Bake meatballs at 325° for 35 to 45 minutes. Serve and eat.

FACTS FACTS FACTS

German scientists have come to the conclusion that the natural distribution of blond hair would cease within the span of 200 years due to the lack of a recessive genes. Only a select amount of people from Sweden and Finland will have naturally blond hair.

Snacks & Desserts

Chicken Salad Sandwich

1 cooked, chicken breast half, chopped
2 stalks celery, chopped
3 tbsp mayonnaise
1/2 onion, diced
2 dill pickles, chopped
1/4 tsp garlic powder
Salt and pepper to taste

Mix together the chicken, celery, mayonnaise, onion and pickle.
Season with the garlic powder, salt and pepper, and stir.
Serve with lettuce on fresh crusty bread or bun.

QUOTES QUOTES QUOTES

"-What kind of sandwich ain't too fattening?
-A half a sandwich."

-Analyze This

Chicken Taco Salad

700 g (1 1/2 lb) cooked chicken breast
2 bunches green onions, sliced
2 1/2 dl (1 cup) sour cream
2 1/2 dl (1 cup) chunky Picante salsa
19 dl (8 cups) tortilla chips

Cut chicken into 1/2 -inch pieces.
In a medium bowl, stir together sour cream and salsa.
Add chicken and 1 cup green onions.
Toss to mix. Make a bed of chips on salad plates,
then spoon salad in center.
Sprinkle remaining green onions on top and serve.

FACTS FACTS FACTS

The first dated account of the taco was written by Bernal Diaz del
Castillo In 1520 in his chronicles called A True History of
the Conquest of New Spain.

Tomato Mozzarella Salad

2 tomatoes, sliced
100 g (3 oz) mozzarella cheese, sliced
1 tbsp balsamic vinegar
5 fresh basil leaves, chopped
2 tbsp olive oil
Salt and pepper
1 clove garlic, crushed

Arrange tomato and mozzarella alternately on platter.
Sprinkle with basil. Combine remaining ingredients and shake well.
Pour over salad and serve.

TRIVIA TRIVIA TRIVIA

The worlds heaviest tomato weighed 3.51 kg (7 lb 12 oz) and was of the cultivar 'Delicious'. It was grown by Gordon Graham of Edmond, Oklahoma in 1986.

Turkey Bacon Sandwich

2 slices white bread
1/2 dl (1/4 cup) mayonnaise
3 lettuce leaves
1 tomato, sliced
3 slices turkey bacon
3 slices Cheddar cheese

Toast the bread slices.
Spread a thin layer of mayonnaise on each slice.
Layer bottom slice with lettuce, tomato, turkey bacon, and cheese.
Spread another thin layer of mayonnaise on the cheese.
Repeat these layers twice. Top with second slice of bread.
Heat in microwave for 45 seconds, or until cheese is melted.

FUN FUN FUN

In the game Six Degrees of Kevin Bacon, players are challenged to link any actor to Kevin Bacon through roles in movies common to both. The number of such links between that actor and Kevin Bacon is known as the actor's Bacon number.

B.L.A.T. Wraps

8 slices bacon
4 flour tortillas
4 tbsp Ranch-style salad dressing
1 avocado, diced
1 tomato, chopped
1 cup lettuce, shredded

Cook bacon until crisp. Drain, crumble, and set aside.
Warm tortillas in microwave oven for 30 to 45 seconds, or until soft. Spread 1 tbsp Ranch dressing down the center of each tortilla. Layer crumbled bacon, avocado, tomato and lettuce over the dressing.
Roll the tortilla and serve.

QUOTES QUOTES QUOTES

"-Hey, I started out mopping the floor just like you guys. But now... now I'm washing lettuce. Soon I'll be on fries; then the grill. And pretty soon, I'll make assistant manager, and that's when the big bucks start rolling in."

-Coming to America

Basil Pesto Sandwich

1 slice focaccia bread, cut in half horizontally
1 tbsp mayonnaise
2 tsp basil pesto
2 tbsp sun-dried tomato pesto
1/2 dl (1/4 cup) red peppers, roasted
1 dl (1/2 cup) feta cheese, crumbled
1 dl (1/2 cup) fresh basil leaves

Mix together mayonnaise and basil pesto and spread onto one half of bread. Spread other half with sun-dried tomato pesto. Arrange roasted red peppers on bottom piece. Cover with feta cheese, then fresh basil.
Top with remaining slice of bread and serve.

FACTS FACTS FACTS

The sandwich was named after John Montagu, 4th Earl of Sandwich, an 18th-century English aristocrat. It is said that Lord Sandwich was fond of this form of food because it allowed him to continue gambling while eating.

BBQ Bacon Cheese Dog

1 beef frank
2 slices bacon, cooked
1 tbsp Cheddar Cheese, shredded
1 hot dog bun
1 tbsp Spicy Cajun Barbecue Sauce
1 tbsp onion, chopped

Place frank, bacon and cheese in bun and wrap in paper towel. Microwave 30 to 45 seconds. Top with barbecue sauce and onion.

FACTS FACTS FACTS

Takeru Kobayashi is the world's fastest hot dog eater. In 2002 he beat his previous record by one half of a hot dog, consuming 50.5 Nathan's famous hot dogs in 12 minutes. On July 4, 2004 he set a new record when he ate 53.5 in the same amount of time. His record has yet to be beat.

Grilled Cheese Sandwich

2 tsp butter
1 slice Cheddar cheese
1 slice Muenster cheese
1 slice Provolone cheese
2 slices rye bread

Preheat your oven's broiler.
Butter one side of each slice of bread, and place butter-side down on a baking sheet. Place cheese slices on top of each piece of bread. Broil until cheese is bubbly and slightly brown. Remove from the oven, and press the two pieces of bread together cheese to cheese.

FACTS FACTS FACTS

The sandwich theorem states that if a real-valued function (the filling) lies everywhere between two other real-valued functions (the bread) which both converge to the same limit, then the "middle function" also converges to that limit.

Cuban
Midnight Sandwich

2 1/2 dl (1 cup) mayonnaise
5 tbsp Italian dressing
4 hoagie rolls, split lengthwise
4 tbsp mustard
200 g (1/2 lb) turkey meat, thinly sliced
200 g (1/2 lb) cooked ham, thinly sliced
200 g (1/2 lb) Swiss cheese, thinly sliced
2 1/2 dl (1 cup) dill pickle slices
1 dl (1/2 cup) olive oil

Mix together mayonnaise and Italian dressing.
Spread on hoagie rolls. Add mustard to each roll. On each roll arrange layers of turkey, ham, and cheese. Top with dill pickle slices.
Close sandwiches, and brush tops and bottoms with olive oil.
Cook sandwiches in a skillet for 2 minutes, pressing down with a plate covered with aluminum foil.
Flip, and cook for 2 more minutes, or until cheese is melted.
Cut in half diagonally and serve.

QUTOES QUOTES QUOTES

"-Sure, Kyle. You can go to the concert after you clean your room, shovel the driveway, and bring democracy to Cuba!"

-South Park

Italian Grilled Cheese Sandwiches

1/2 dl (1/4 cup) butter
1/8 tsp garlic powder
12 slices white bread
1 tsp dried oregano
1 (200 g / 8 oz) package shredded mozzarella cheese
1 jar Picante sauce

Preheat your oven's broiler. Place 6 slices of bread onto a baking sheet. Spread a small handful of mozzarella cheese over each slice. Top with the remaining 6 slices of bread. Mix together butter and garlic powder, and brush some over the tops of the sandwiches, or spread with the back of a tablespoon.
Sprinkle with dried oregano. Cook under broiler for 2 to 3 minutes, or until golden brown. Remove sandwiches from oven, flip over and brush the other sides with butter. Sprinkle with oregano and return to the broiler. Cook until golden, about 2 minutes. Cut sandwiches in half diagonally, and serve with Picante sauce on the side for dipping.

QUOTES QUOTES QUOTES

"-Someday, you'll be known as the Italian Stallion."

-The Italian Stallion

Peanut Butter and Apple Sandwich

2 slices whole wheat bread
1 tbsp peanut butter
1 apple – peeled and shredded

Spread a thin layer of peanut butter onto one side of each slice of bread. Place shredded apple onto the peanut butter, and place the other peanut buttered side of bread on top.

FACTS FACTS FACTS

As of September 2004, the most expensive peanut butter on the market is a $532 limited item which can be mail-ordered from the National Institute of Standards and Technology (NIST) of the United States. This peanut butter (SRM 2387) is a set of three 6 oz (170 g) jars which will expire on December 31, 2009.

Reuben Sandwich

8 slices rye bread
1 1/2 dl (3/4 cup) Thousand Island dressing
1 (450 g / 16 oz) can sauerkraut, drained
8 slices Swiss cheese
8 slices pastrami
1/2 dl (1/4 cup) butter

Spread each slice of bread with Thousand Island dressing.
Top 4 pieces of bread with sauerkraut, cheese and pastrami.
Place remaining bread slices, one on each piece of bread.
Spread margarine on the outsides of each sandwich.
Heat a large skillet over medium high heat.
Grill until browned, then turn and grill until heated through
and cheese is melted.

TRIVIA TRIVIA TRIVIA

The Reuben Awards, named for Rube Goldberg, are presented each year
by the National Cartoonists Society to the person chosen as Cartoonist
of the Year. 2002's winner, for example, was Matt Groening.

Bagel Pizza

1 bagel, sliced in half
1 dl (1/2 cup) tomato sauce
1/2 dl (1/4 cup) mozzarella cheese, shredded
1 small onion, sliced
1 green bell pepper, chopped
1 package sliced pepperoni sausage

Preheat toaster oven to 425 degrees F (220 degrees C).
Spread bottom bagel half with tomato sauce. Add cheese,
onion, bell pepper and pepperoni. Place other half of bagel
on top. Place bagel in oven and toast about 10 minutes, or
until bagel is golden brown. Serve.

QUOTES QUOTES QUOTES

"-I'm going to microwave a bagel and have sex with it."

-Family Guy

Tuna Pita Melts

6 pitas
2 cans tuna
2 tbsp mayonnaise
2 tbsp dill pickle relish
1/2 tsp dried dill
1/4 tsp salt
1 tomato, sliced
2 1/2 dl (1 cup) Cheddar cheese, shredded

Preheat oven to 400 degrees F (200 degrees C).
Bake whole pitas for 5 minutes, or until lightly toasted.
Mix tuna, mayonnaise, relish, dill and salt together.
Spread an equal amount onto each of the pita breads.
Arrange tomato wedges over the tuna, and sprinkle with shredded
Cheddar cheese. Bake for 5 minutes in oven, or until cheese has
melted.

TRIVIA TRIVIA TRIVIA

A Dolphin is a Prince Albert piercing attached to another, deeper Prince
Albert piercing. Its name comes from the appearance of the jewelry
"diving" through the surface of the skin.

Crab Dip

1/2 green bell pepper, chopped
1 onion, chopped
3 tbsp butter
350 g (12 oz) imitation crabmeat
2 1/2 dl (1 cup) mayonnaise

Sauté the green pepper and onion in butter for 3 minutes, or until vegetables are tender. Stir in crabmeat, and sauté for another 3 minutes. Remove from heat.
Put crabmeat mixture into a medium bowl.
Stir in mayonnaise.
Serve warm or chilled.

QUOTES QUOTES QUOTES

"-You wait till you've given them crabs.
Then you'll really know hatred."

-Cocktail

BBQ Chicken
Sandwich with Cheese

1 dl (1/2 cup) onion, sliced
1 dl (1/2 cup) green pepper strips
1 tbsp oil
4 chicken breast halves
1 dl (1/3 cup) barbecue sauce
8 cheese slices
4 Kaiser rolls, split, toasted

Cook and stir onion and green pepper in oil in skillet on medium heat until tender. Brush both sides of chicken breasts with barbecue sauce.
Broil 6 to 7 minutes on each side or until cooked through.
Top each chicken breast with 2 cheese slices. Broil until melted.
Fill rolls with chicken and top with onion and green pepper.

FACTS FACTS FACTS

"Drunken chicken" is the name given to any preparation of chicken that involves alcoholic beverages.

Chicken Caesar Pita

2 chicken breast halves, cooked and cut into thin strips
7 dl (3 cups) lettuce, torn into pieces
1/2 dl (1/4 cup) Parmesan cheese, grated
1 dl (1/2 cup) garlic salad dressing
2 pita breads, cut in half

Mix chicken, lettuce, cheese and dressing.
Spoon evenly into pita bread halves.

TRIVIA TRIVIA TRIVIA

The Caesar cut is a man's hairstyle with a short, horizontally straight cut fringe. The hair is layered to around 1 to 2 inches all over. It is named after Julius Caesar. For youths of the 1990s, it is also called a Clooney cut, because it was worn by actor George Clooney on the TV show ER.

Crab Muffins

100 g (3 oz) cream cheese
1 tbsp milk
2 tsp lemon juice
Dash of hot sauce
2 green onions, chopped
2 1/2 dl (1 cup) crab meat
2 English muffins.

Beat cream cheese with milk, lemon juice and hot sauce.
Mix in green onions and crab meat.
Split and butter 2 English muffins.
Toast under broiler. Spread filling on toasted muffins and place
under broiler until slightly browned.

QUOTES QUOTES QUOTES

"-Kelso, women are like muffins, man. And once you've had a muffin,
you will put up with ANYTHING to have another one.
And they know that."

-That´70s Show

Snickers Pie

8 Snickers bars
100 g (4 oz) chocolate
1 tbsp Bailey's Irish Creme liqueur
1 egg, separated
1 tbsp sugar
5 dl (2 cups) whipping cream

Chop 7 of the Snickers bars and press into the bottom of a greased pie pan for the crust. Chop and reserve the remaining bar. Melt chocolate over hot water or in the microwave.
Stir in liqueur. Beat in egg yolk. In a bowl, whip egg whites and gradually add sugar until it holds a stiff peak.
Fold in chocolate mixture. Whip cream and fold 2/3 of it into the chocolate mixture. Spread chocolate mixture on top of pie crust.
Garnish with remaining whipped cream and the last Snickers.
Refrigerate until ready to serve.

FACTS FACTS FACTS

Snickers is the best selling candy bar of all time
and has annual global sales of $2 billion.

Heavenly Hash

1 small box instant vanilla pudding
1 can crushed pineapple
2-3 handfuls miniature marshmallows
1 can fruit cocktail
250 g (1 9-oz) Cool Whip

Mix pineapple, including juice, with pudding mix.
Drain fruit cocktail.
Add other ingredients.
Stir together.
Chill before serving.

QUTOES QUOTES QUOTES

"-What's wrong?
-She saw a mouse.
-She saw a mouse? In here?
-No. Before. Outside. But she relives it."

-Heaven Can Wait

M & M Cheesecake Squares

1/2 dl (1/4 cup) margarine
2 1/2 dl (1 cup) unbleached all-purpose flour
200 g (8 oz) cream cheese, softened
1 tsp vanilla
1 1/2 dl (3/4 cup) M&M candies
1 dl (1/3 cup) packed brown sugar
1 dl (1/2 cup) walnuts, chopped
1/2 dl (1/4 cup) granulated sugar
1 large egg

Beat margarine and brown sugar until light and fluffy.
Add flour and walnuts, mix well. Reserve 1 dl (1/2 cup) crumb mixture. Press remaining crumb mixture into bottom of 20 cm (8 inch) square pan. Bake at 350°F for 10 minutes.
Combine cream cheese, granulated sugar and vanilla, mix until well blended. Add egg, mix well. Layer 1 dl (1/2 cup) candy over crust and top with cream cheese mixture. Combine remaining candy, chopped, and reserved crumb mixture and mix well. Sprinkle crumb mixture over cream cheese. Bake at 350°F for 20 minutes. Cool and cut in to 16 equal squares.

FUN FUN FUN

The rock band Van Halen's now infamous performance contract called for, among other things, a bowl of M&M's backstage, but with a provision that all the brown candies must be removed. The M&M's clause was included in Van Halen's contracts not as an act of caprice, but to provide an easy way of determining whether the technical specifications of the contract had been thoroughly read.

Peanut Butter Squares

250 g (2 sticks) margarine
6 dl (2 1/2 cups) sugar
2 1/2 dl (1 cup) smooth peanut butter
4 dl (1 3/4 cup) graham cracker crumbs
1 pkg (350 g / 12 oz) chocolate chips

Melt margarine. Remove from heat and add peanut butter, sugar and graham cracker crumbs. Mix well. Spread in ungreased pan. Press down evenly. Melt chocolate chips and spread over top of peanut butter mixture.
Chill for 25 minutes, then cut in small squares.

QUOTES QUOTES QUOTES

"-The cat won't fit in the toaster. Never mind, I'll make a peanut butter sandwich, where's the blender?"

-ALF

Buster Bars

1 package chocolate sandwich cookies
1 dl (1/2 cup) margarine
1 jar dry roasted peanuts
2 l (1/2 gallon) vanilla ice cream
5 1/2 dl (2 1/4 cup) powdered sugar
1 1/2 dl (2/3 cup) chocolate chips
1 dl (1/2 cup) margarine
3 1/2 dl (1 1/2 cup) evaporated milk

Crush cookies, melt margarine and mix together. Pat into 23x33 cm (9x13 inch) pan and put in freezer until hard. Slice ice cream onto crust, cover with peanuts and return to freezer. In a pot, cook powdered sugar, chocolate chips, margarine, and evaporated milk, for about 8 minutes, stirring constantly. Remove from heat and cool. Once it's cool, pour it over the frozen crust. Keep in freezer until ready to eat.

TRIVIA TRIVIA TRIVIA

One of the most famous Busters helped execute The Great Train Robbery. The Royal Mail's Glasgow to London traveling post office train was stopped by tampered signals. The 15-member gang got away with £2.6 million. One of the gang members, Ronald "Buster" Edwards, fled to Mexico but later surrendered to authorities. Edwards became a flower seller outside Waterloo Station on his release from prison. He committed suicide in 1994.

Chocolate Pudding

1/2 dl (1/4 cup) sugar
2 tbsp cornstarch
5 dl (2 cups) hot milk
100 g (3 oz) chocolate, chopped
1 tsp vanilla extract

Stir sugar and cornstarch together in medium saucepan.
Gradually stir in milk. Heat, stirring constantly, until sugar dissolves
and mixture begins to boil and thicken, about 10 minutes.
Add chocolate. Cook until chocolate is melted and mixture
thickens--about 5 minutes. Remove from heat and let it cool for 5
minutes. Stir in vanilla. Pour into small custard cups. Serve warm
or at room temperature.

QUOTES QUOTES QUOTES

"-You can go to places in the world with pudding. That's funny."

-Punch-Drunk Love

Double Cherry Crunch

2 cans cherry pie filling
1/2 tsp almond extract
5 dl (2 cups) sugar
5 dl (2 cups) sifted flour
2 tsp baking powder
2 eggs
2 tbsp butter

Spread cans of cherry pie filling across the bottom of a baking pan. Sprinkle the almond extract over pie filling. In a bowl, beat eggs. Mix in sugar, flour, and baking powder. Combine until moist and crumbly. Spread this topping over the cherries. Melt butter and pour over all. Bake for 40 minutes in a 350°F. oven.
Serve with whipping cream or vanilla ice cream.

FACTS FACTS FACTS

Sakura is the Japanese name for ornamental cherry trees and their blossoms. Cherry blossoms are an enduring metaphor for the ephemeral nature of life, and as such are frequently depicted in art, and are associated with both samurai and kamikaze.

Blueberry Focaccia

1 dl (1/2 cup) butter, melted
900 g (2 lb) frozen bread dough, defrosted
7 dl (3 cups) fresh or frozen blueberries
1 1/2 dl (3/4 cup) sugar

Brush a 35 cm (14-inch) pizza pan with some of the melted butter. Press bread loaves together and roll out with a rolling pin. Press dough in pizza pan with your fingers, making an even flat surface to the rim. Press fingertips into top of dough, making indentations. Drizzle with remaining butter. Evenly sprinkle top with blueberries, then with sugar. Gently press into dough to adhere.
Cover loosely with plastic wrap and let rest at room temperature 30 minutes. Fifteen minutes before baking, preheat the oven to 350°F.
Bake in center of oven until golden brown, about 30 minutes. Cut into wedges and serve with cream cheese.

QUOTES QUOTES QUOTES

"-I'll be back before you can say blueberry pie.
-Blueberry pie.
-OK, maybe not that fast..."

-Pulp Fiction

Very Difficult Muffins

2 tbsp vegetable oil
6 dl (2 1/2 cups) all-purpose flour
2 tsp baking powder
1 tsp baking soda
1/2 tsp salt
1 tsp ground cinnamon
3 dl (1 1/3 cups) granulated sugar
4 eggs
3 dl (1 1/4 cups) oil
1 tbsp vanilla extract
3 carrots, grated
1 large apple, peeled and chopped
1 dl (1/3 cup) raisins
1 dl (1/3 cup) sweetened flaked coconut
1 dl (1/3 cup) pecans, chopped
15 muffin cups

Preheat oven to 375°F.

In a bowl, mix the flour, baking powder, baking soda, salt and cinnamon. In a separate bowl, whisk the sugar, eggs, oil and vanilla. Add the carrots, apple, raisins, coconut and pecans to the egg mixture and stir well to combine. Add the flour mixture and stir until blended. Do not overmix. Scoop batter into muffin cups. The batter should be thick enough to mound slightly above the muffin pan line. Bake 25 to 30 minutes or until a toothpick inserted in the center of the muffin comes out clean.

FACTS FACTS FACTS

Unsolved Math Problem:
Is P equal to NP?

Brownies for Dummies

5 dl (2 cups) miniature marshmallows
5 dl (2 cups) chocolate morsels
2 1/2 dl (1 cup) pecans, chopped
2 1/2 dl (1 cup) evaporated milk
2 1/2 dl (1 cup) sifted powdered sugar
7 dl (3 cups) vanilla wafer crumbs
1/2 tsp salt
2 tsp evaporated milk

Put chocolate morsels and 2 1/2 dl (1 cup) milk into a saucepan. Stir over low heat until chocolate melts. Remove from heat. In a bowl, mix the vanilla wafer crumbs, marshmallows, pecans, powdered sugar and salt. Reserve 1/2 chocolate mixture for glaze and stir the rest into crumb mixture. Mix well. Press into greased 23 cm (9-inch) square pan. Stir 2 tsp milk into reserved 1 dl (1/2 cup) chocolate mixture and spread evenly over mixture in pan. Chill until glaze is set. Cut into squares and serve.

TRIVIA TRIVIA TRIVIA

"Brownie points" are a hypothetical currency which can be accrued by doing good deeds or earning favor in the eyes of another, often one's superior.

Peanut Butter Cookies

1/2 dl (1/4 cup) cocoa
2 1/2 dl (1 cup) peanut butter
1 dl (1/2 cup) margarine
1 1/2 tsp vanilla
1 dl (1/2 cup) milk
1/2 tsp salt
5 dl (2 cups) sugar
7 - 9 1/2 dl (3 - 4 cups) uncooked quick oats
3 1/2 dl (1 1/2 cups) pecans, chopped

Melt butter in a saucepan. Add milk, sugar and cocoa and stir until dissolved. Let bubble 1 minute then stir in peanut butter and vanilla. Add oatmeal and leave to cool. Add nuts and beat until thick. Distribute spoonfuls onto cookie sheet.
Leave until dry.

QUOTES QUOTES QUOTES

"-Yeah, I know. A week ago, I was at the planetarium, and as they were leaving I sold like 50 boxes. That's when I realized what sells a lot of these - munchies. After that, I started hitting NYU dorms around midnight. They call me "Cookie Duuuude"."

-Friends

Chicken Fajita Dip

2 blocks cream cheese
1 pkg taco seasoning
5 dl (2 cups) chicken, chopped
1 bottle taco sauce
5 dl (2 cups) cheddar cheese, shredded
Lettuce, chopped
Tomatoes, chopped
Jalapeno slices
Black olive slices

Mix taco seasoning and cream cheese together. Spread in a baking dish and top with chicken. Cover with coating of taco sauce and cover with shredded cheese. Place in 350° F. oven for about 20 minutes, or until cheese is bubbly. Garnish with chopped lettuce, tomatoes, jalapenos, olives. Serve with tortilla chips.

TRIVIA TRIVIA TRIVIA

Butchers along the Texas border with Mexico used the word fajita to refer to the diaphragm muscle of a steer. The cut is known in the US as the skirt steak, and it remains popular for making fajitas.

Artichoke Bacon Dip

1 can artichoke hearts, chopped
4 pieces bacon, cooked & crumbled
1 tbsp onion, minced
1 tbsp lemon juice
1 dl (1/2 cup) mayonnaise
1 dash cayenne pepper
Salt and pepper to taste
Worcestershire sauce to taste

Mix all ingredients and refrigerate overnight.
Serve with crackers or tortilla chips.

FACTS FACTS FACTS

The Jerusalem artichoke has absolutely nothing to do with Jerusalem,
and little to do with true artichokes. When cooked it gives them a
legendary facility to produce flatulence.

Bacon and Cheddar Dip

1 package Ranch party dip
1 package sour cream
1/2 dl (1/4 cup) bacon bits
2 1/2 dl (1 cup) cheddar cheese, shredded

Mix party dip with sour cream.
Add bacon bits and cheese.
Mix together and serve.

FACTS FACTS FACTS

Cheddar is a village in the district of Sedgemoor in Somerset, England,
situated on the edge of the Mendip Hills nine miles north west of Wells.
The village has a population of 5,724 (2002 estimate) and it is famous
for having given its name to Cheddar cheese.

Black Bean Dip

1 can black beans
1 tsp chili powder
1/4 tsp salt
1/4 tsp black pepper
1/4 tsp ground cumin
2 drops hot pepper sauce
1 1/2 dl (3/4 cup) onion, minced
2 cloves garlic, minced
100 g (4 oz) green chiles, chopped

Drain beans, reserving 2 tbsp liquid. Combine beans, chili powder, salt, black pepper, cumin, hot pepper sauce and liquid from beans in blender or food processor. Process till smooth.
Cook onion and garlic over low heat till onion is slightly browned. Add chilies and cook 3 minutes more.
Add bean mixture and mix well.

QUOTES QUOTES QUOTES

"-If you're going to become true dodgeballers, then you've got to learn the five D's of dodgeball: Dodge, Duck, Dip, Dive and Dodge!

-Dodgeball: A True Underdog Story

Creamy Chipotle Dip

2 canned chipotle peppers, mashed
2 1/2 dl (1 cup) mayonnaise
1 tbsp lime juice
1 dl (1/2 cup) sour cream
1/4 tsp garlic salt
1/2 dl (1/4 cup) onions, chopped
1 tbsp fresh cilantro, chopped
Tortilla chips

In small bowl, combine all ingredients except chips.
Serve with chips or your favorite dippers.

FACTS FACTS FACTS

The substances that gives chile peppers their heat is capsaicin. Capsaicin is the primary ingredient in pepper spray. The "heat" of chile peppers is measured in Scoville units. Bell peppers rank at zero Scoville units. The record for the highest number of Scoville units in a chile pepper is assigned by the Guinness Book of Records to the Red Savina Habanero, measuring 577,000 units. Pure capsaicin rates at 16,000,000 Scoville units.

Blue Cheese Dip

1 package cream cheese
1 package blue cheese
2 tbsp chives, chopped
1 tsp dill weed
1 tsp salt
1/4 tsp garlic powder
1 can crushed pineapple

Beat cheese together. Add all seasonings and blend.
Fold in pineapple with juice. Chill 1 to 2 hours and serve
with raw vegetables or chips.

FACTS FACTS FACTS

Blue Cheese was originally made by farmers who would collect the milk,
curdle it with rennet, then scoop the curds by hand into molds.
A powder made from grating moldy bread was sprinkled into the curds . . .
The bread was stored in the same damp caves that aged the cheese, and
in a few weeks it turned blue and was ground to dust for cheese making.

California Mexican Hot Dip

2 bunches green onions, chopped
1 small jar green olives, chopped
1/2 dl (1/4 cup) green bell pepper, chopped
Lettuce, sliced
2 cans refried beans
1 package taco seasoning
200 g (1/2 lb) cheddar cheese, grated
2 packages frozen avocado dip
4 tbsp sour cream
1 small can green chilies
2 tomatoes, quartered
Chips
Hot sauce

In a small bowl, mix the chopped green onions, olives, and green bell pepper.
In another bowl, mix refried beans with the taco seasoning.
Layer lettuce slices, bean mixture, vegetables, tomatoes, and grated cheese. Serve with chips and hot sauce.

QUOTES QUOTES QUOTES

"-Hola.
-I no fuck around, comprende? Gun, gun,
loaded. Bang, bang. You dead.
-Do you have a speech impediment?"

-The Mexican

Green Herb Dip

1 1/2 dl (3/4 cup) yogurt
1/2 dl (1/4 cup) mayonnaise
1/4 tsp salt
1 dl (1/2 cup) watercress
1 dl (1/2 cup) fresh parsley
1/2 dl (1/4 cup) fresh basil
1 green onion, chopped

Place yogurt, mayonnaise and salt in blender.
Add remaining ingredients.
Blend on high speed about 30 seconds, until finely chopped.
Cover and refrigerate about 1 hour.
Serve with raw vegetables or chips.

QUOTES QUOTES QUOTES

"-What is the different types of hash out there? We all know that it's called the bionic, the bomb, the puff, the blow, the black, the herb, the sensie, the cronic, the sweet Mary Jane, the shit, Ganja, split, reefa, the bad, the buddha, the home grown, the ill, the maui-maui, the method, pot, lethal turbo, tie, shake, skunk, stress, whacky, weed, glaze, the boot, dimebag, Scooby Doo, bob, bogey, back yard boogie. But what is the other terms for it?"

-Ali G

Curry Garlic Veggie Dip

1 pint mayonnaise
3 tbsp chili sauce
1 tbsp curry powder
1 tbsp garlic powder
1/4 tsp salt
1/4 tsp pepper
1 tbsp grated onion
1 tbsp Worcestershire sauce

Combine all ingredients in a large bowl and mix well.
Cover and refrigerate over night, allowing the flavors to blend together. Serve with raw vegetables or chips.

FACTS FACTS FACTS

One of the largest concentrations of Indian restaurants outside the Indian subcontinent can be found on the "Curry Mile" in Rusholme, Manchester, UK.

Chili Cheese Ball

1 package cream cheese
1 block Cheddar cheese, shredded
2 tbsp milk
2 garlic cloves, minced
1 package chili seasoning
2 1/2 dl (1 cup) walnuts, chopped

In food processor or with mixer, blend softened cream cheese, shredded cheddar, milk and garlic until smooth. Chill for 1/2 hour. Put the chili mix seasoning on a plate and the chopped nuts on another. Form the cheese into ball shape with your hands, then roll in chili seasoning, covering completely, then roll in nuts. Refrigerate until about an hour before serving. Serve with crackers.

QUOTES QUOTES QUOTES

"-I want a helmet. A cheese helmet. A helmet full of cheese. You just pop it on your head and eat all day. I want it all, folks. I want it all and I want it now and I'm gonna get it with or without your help. I think you know what I'm talking about. I think you hear me knocking and I think I'm coming in and you know what? I'm already wearing the cheese helmet."

-Denis Leary

Taco Pizza

2 cans refrigerated crescent rolls
200 g (8 oz) cream cheese
200 g (8 oz) sour cream
1 package taco seasoning
1 tomato, chopped
Black olives, sliced
Green onions, chopped
200 g (8 oz) Cheddar cheese, shredded

Spread crescent rolls in a 25x40 cm (10x15 inch) pan, sealing all seams.
Bake until golden.
Mix cream cheese, sour cream, and taco seasoning until creamy.
Top with tomato, olives, green onions and cheddar.
Refrigerate to blend flavors.

FACTS FACTS FACTS

The World Pizza Championship is an event held every year to determine the world's best pizza makers. It is organized by the magazine "Pizza e Pasta Italiana". Pizzas are judged by preparation, taste, and proper cooking. Pizza competitions include: acrobatics, speed, freestyle, and size. Salsomaggiore Terme (Parma), Italy, is the site of the 2006 championships.

Beef Tortillas

2 1/2 dl (1 cup) sour cream
2 tbsp prepared horseradish
1 tbsp Dijon-style mustard
5 flour tortillas
30 fresh spinach leaves
10 thin slices deli roast beef
2 1/2 dl (1 cup) Cheddar cheese, shredded

Stir together sour cream, horseradish and mustard.
Spread 3 tbsp of mixture evenly on each tortilla.
Arrange 5 or 6 spinach leaves over sour cream mixture.
Place 2 slices roast beef over spinach. Sprinkle with 3 tbsp cheese.
Roll each tortilla up tightly.
To serve, cut each tortilla diagonally in half.

QUOTES QUOTES QUOTES

"-Sweets. You couldn't ignore me if you tried. So... so. Are you guys like
boyfriend-girlfriend? Steady dates? Lovers? Come on, Sporto,
level with me. Do you slip her the hot beef injection?"

-The Breakfast Club

Bruschetta

1 large ready-to-eat pizza crust
2 cloves garlic, chopped
2 1/2 dl (1 cup) tomato, diced
8 fresh basil leaves, sliced
Salt and pepper to taste
2 1/2 dl (1 cup) Mozzarella cheese, shredded

Preheat oven to 375° F. Toss together cheese, garlic, tomato, basil, salt and pepper. Spread mixture on top of bread. Bake for 8-10 minutes or until cheese is melted. Cut in slices, serve immediately.

QUOTES QUOTES QUOTES

"-I'm not Latin, I'm Italian."

-Joey

Spinach Bars
(VEGGIE)

50 g (1/2 stick) butter
2 packages frozen spinach, chopped, thawed and squeezed dry
3 eggs
1 tsp baking powder
6 mushrooms, chopped
1 onion, minced
1 tsp salt
450 g (1 lb) Cheddar cheese, grated

Melt butter in 23x33 cm (9x13 inch) baking dish.
In a bowl, combine spinach, eggs, baking powder, mushrooms,
onion, salt and cheese.
Pour in dish and bake at 350 F for 35 minutes.
Cool before cutting into cubes.

TRIVIA TRIVIA TRIVIA

The longest bar in the world is 684 feet, or about 208.5 meters
long, and is located at the New Bulldog in Rock Island, Illinois.

Hummus

3 large garlic cloves
2 cans garbanzo beans (chickpeas), drained
1 lemon
1 dl (1/2 cup) olive oil
1/2 tsp salt
1/4 tsp black pepper

Put the peeled garlic and garbanzo beans in a blender. Cut the lemon in half and squeeze the juice in the blender along with half of the olive oil. Start blending to chop up the beans. Stop once in a while to stir with a spoon.
Add the rest of the olive oil and blend until smooth.
Add salt and pepper.

Use as a spread for sandwiches or serve with pita bread or nachos.

FACTS FACTS FACTS

Quite a few English words are ultimately derived from Arabic, often through other European languages. Among them every-day vocabulary like "sugar", "cotton", "magazine", "algebra", "alcohol" and "zenith".

Guacamole

3 large ripe avocados
1 red onion, diced
3 tbsp chopped fresh cilantro
2 tsp seeded and minced fresh jalapeno
1/2 lime
1/2 tsp salt

Cut the avocado lengtwise and split it in two pieces.
Use a spoon and scoop out the flesh and place it in
a medium bowl. Mash lightly with a fork.
Stir in the red onion, cilantro and jalapeno.
Squeeze the lime over the mix and stir in the salt.

Serve with tortilla chips or regular chips.

QUOTES QUOTES QUOTES

"-Holy Guacamole! This looks like a job for Wonder Pig."

-The Muppet Show

Tomato Salsa

2 medium-sized ripe tomatoes
1 small onion, diced
3 tbsp chopped fresh cilantro
2 tsp seeded and minced fresh jalapeno
1 tsp olive oil
1/4 tsp salt
1/2 lime

Cut the cores out of the tomatoes, cut them in half and remove the seeds. Dice them and put in a medium bowl. Add the onion, cilantro, jalapeno, olive oil and salt and stir.
Squeeze the lime over the mixture.

Serve with tortilla chips or regular chips.

FUN FUN FUN

Salsa is danced on music with a recurring eight-beat pattern, i.e. two bars of four beats. Salsa patterns typically use three steps during each four beats, one beat being skipped. However, this skipped beat is often marked by a tap, a kick, a flick, etc. Salsa music is fast with around 180 beats per minute.

French Toast

3 large eggs
1 dl (1/3 cup) milk
1/4 tsp vanilla extract
Pinch of salt
2 tbsp butter
4 slices bread
Powdered sugar
Maple syrup

Use a fork and beat the eggs with milk,
vanilla and salt in a small bowl.
Melt butter in a skillet over medium heat.
Dip and soak the bread in the mixture and place in the hot skillet.
Flip the slices over once they turn golden and cook on other side.
Transfer to a plate. Powder with sugar and serve with maple syrup.

QUOTES QUOTES QUOTES

"-A man may fight for many things: his country, his principles, his friends,
the glistening tear on the cheek of a golden child. But personally I'd
mud-wrestle my own mother for a ton of cash, an amusing clock
and a sack of French porn."

-Blackadder the Third

Flapjacks

2 1/2 dl (1 cup) flour
2 tbsp sugar
1/2 tsp baking soda
1/4 tsp salt
2 eggs
2 1/2 dl (1 cup) buttermilk
1 tsp vanilla extract
3 tbsp vegetable oil
3 tbsp butter
Butter
Maple syrup

In a small bowl, mix together flour, sugar, baking soda and salt.
Use a fork and beat the eggs with buttermilk and vanilla in a small
bowl. Heat a large skillet over medium heat. Add 1 tbsp oil and
1 tbsp butter.
Ladle butter into the skillet using a 1 dl (1/3-cup) measure.
Cook until the undersides are golden.
Flip the pancakes and cook the other side.
Serve with butter and maple syrup.

FACTS FACTS FACTS

Pancake Day or Pancake Tuesday is the name by which Shrove
Tuesday is also known in Britain, Ireland, and Australia.

Grilled Cheese Sandwich

1 tbsp butter
2 slices white bread
1 dl (1/2 cup) shredded cheddar or jack cheese

Heat a large skillet over medium heat.
Butter both sides of the bread and cook, on both sides, in the skillet until golden.
Place the cheese on one of the bread slices and top with the other slice. Cook until the cheese is melted.

TRIVIA TRIVIA TRIVIA

On 23 November 2004, the Virgin Mary grilled cheese sandwich was sold for $28,000 in an eBay auction. Diana Duyser claimed to see the Virgin Mary toasted into the bread in 1994 and sealed it into a plastic bag.

Coleslaw

1 dl (1/2 cup) mayonnaise
3 tbsp vinegar
2 tsp sugar
1/4 tsp salt
Pinch of black pepper
1 (200 g / 8 oz) bag coleslaw mix or shredded cabbage

Mix mayo, vinegar, sugar, salt and pepper in a large bowl.
Add the coleslaw mix and stir to combine.

QUOTES QUOTES QUOTES

"-What in the name of Aunt Eileen's cabbageless coleslaw is going on?"

-The Angry Beavers

Chocolate Chip Cookies

2 1/2 dl (1 cup) all-purpose flour
1/2 tsp baking soda
1/2 tsp salt
1 dl (1/2 cup) butter
1 dl (1/2 cup) brown sugar
1 dl (1/3 cup) sugar
1 large egg
1/2 tsp vanilla extract
150 g (2 1/2 dl / 1 cup) chocolate chips
1 dl (1/2 cup) chopped walnuts

Heat the oven to 375 degrees F (190 degrees C).
Combine flour, baking soda and salt in a small bowl.
In a large bowl, mix butter, brown sugar, sugar, egg and vanilla until creamy. Add flour mixture and stir. Then add chocolate chips and walnuts. Dop walnut-sized balls of dough onto a baking sheet. Bake until golden, for 9 to 11 minutes.

FACTS FACTS FACTS

The chocolate-chip cookie was accidentally developed by Ruth Graves Wakefield, in 1937. Wakefield was making chocolate cookies but ran out of regular baker's chocolate and substituted broken pieces of semi-sweet chocolate, assuming it would melt and mix into the batter. It did not, and the cookie with chips of chocolate was born.

Apple Oatmeal

1 dl (1/2 cup) rolled oats
1 dl (1/2 cup) milk
1 dl (1/2 cup) water
2 tbsp raisins
1/2 tbsp brown sugar
1/2 apple, chopped
Pinch of salt
Cinnamon

Mix oats, milk, water, raisins, brown sugar, apple and salt
in a saucepan. Bring to boil and let simmer for 7 minutes.
Serve with cinnamon.

FUN FUN FUN

The 12th Annual World Porridge Making Championships took take place
in Carrbridge, Inverness-shire, Scotland, on Sunday 9th October 2005.
Winner, and World Porridge Champion, was Lynn Benge.

Hummus Sandwich

2 tbsp hummus
1 pita pocket
4 slices cucumber
Handful of bean sprouts
Handful of chopped green or red peppers

Spread hummus in the pita pocket.
Slide in cucumber,
sproutes and peppers.

TRIVIA TRIVIA TRIVIA

The inner temperature of a cucumber can be up
to 20 degrees cooler than the outside air.

Tomato and Grilled Cheese Sandwich

1 slice cheddar cheese
2 slices bread
1 slice tomato
Basil to taste
1 tsp butter

Lay the cheese on one slice of the bread.
Top with tomato, basil and the second bread slice.
Melt the butter in a skillet.
Cook the sandwich until golden, about 2 minutes on each side.

FACTS FACTS FACTS

The tomato is the world's most popular fruit. Just like the pumpkin, botanically speaking it is a fruit, not a vegetable. More than 60 million tons of tomatoes are produced per year.

Tuna Muffin

2 English muffins, split in half
1 can tuna, drained
1 1/2 tbsp mayonnaise
Salt and pepper to taste
1/2 dl (1/4 cup) cheddar cheese, shredded

Heat the oven to 350 degrees F (180 degrees C).
Toast the muffins in a toaster. Mix the tuna, mayo, salt and pepper and spread it eavenly over each muffin half. Sprinkle cheese on top and bake in oven until cheese has melted.

TRIVIA TRIVIA TRIVIA

Dunkin' Donuts created the "World's Largest Muffin", an edible treat that was 500 pounds, seven feet tall, four feet wide and contained 30 pounds of blueberries.

Whole Wheat Biscuits with Honey

2 1/2 dl (1 cup) lukewarm water
2 tbsp active dry yeast
5 tsp honey
6 dl (2 1/2 cups) whole wheat flour
Vegetable oil

Pour the water into a bowl and stir in the yeast. Let it sit for a couple of minutes then add honey and flour, and mix well. Grease a muffin tin with the oil and fill each cup halfway with batter.
Heat the oven to 350 degrees F (180 degrees C).
Cover the tin with a towel and let it sit for 30-40 minutes.
Bake for 20 minutes and let it sit in the tins for 5 minutes before removing.

QUOTES QUOTES QUOTES

"-I love you, Pumpkin.
-I love you too, Honey Bunny.
-Alright, everybody be cool, this is a robbery! Any of you fucking pricks move, and I'll execute every motherfucking last one of ya!"

-Pulp Fiction

Beer Bread

7 dl (3 cups) all-purpose flour
3 tbsp sugar
4 tbsp active dry yeast
1 bottle of beer
Vegetable oil

Combine the flour, sugar and yeast in a large bowl.
Add the beer and mix well.
Grease a loaf pan with oil and pour in the batter.
Place in a cold oven and set it to 350 degrees F
(180 degrees C). Bake for 40-45 minutes.
Let it cool before removing it from the pan.

FACTS FACTS FACTS

Beer is one of the oldest beverages humans have produced, dating back
to at least the 5th millennium BC and recorded in the written history of
Ancient Egypt and Mesopotamia.

Chocolate Chip Muffins gone Banana

1 dl (1/2 cup) vegetable shortening
2 1/2 dl (1 cup) sugar
5 dl (2 cups) all-purpose flour
2 eggs
1/2 tsp salt
3 large bananas
1 tsp baking soda
1 tsp baking powder
1 1/2 dl (2/3 cup) mini chocolate chips

Heat the oven to 350 degrees F (180 degrees C). Mix shortening and sugar in a bowl. Add a tablespoon flour to the mixture. Beat in eggs one at a time. Mash the bananas on a plate. Set aside 1 dl (1/2 cup) flour and add the rest and the banana to the mixture. Mix well. In another bowl, mix the remaining flour with salt, baking soda, baking powder and chocolate chips. Stir together both the mixtures and pour the batter into greased muffin tins and bake for 25 minutes.

TRIVIA TRIVIA TRIVIA

A banana plant is an herb, which because of its size and structure, is often mistaken for a tree. Globally, bananas rank fourth after rice, wheat and maize in human consumption.

Peanut Butter Cookies

4 tbsp butter
1 1/2 dl (3/4 cup) brown sugar
1 1/2 dl (3/4 cup) peanut butter
1 egg
1/2 dl (1/4 cup) applesauce
1 tsp vanilla extract
3 1/2 dl (1 1/2 cups) flour
3/4 tsp baking soda

Heat the oven to 375 degrees F (190 degrees C).
Mix butter, brown sugar and peanut butter in a bowl.
Stir in applesauce, vanilla and egg.
Combine flour and baking soda in a separate bowl. Gradually add it to the wet ingredients. Mix thoroughly. Drop spoonfuls of dough onto an ungreased cookie sheet and press each piece with a fork. Bake for 8 minutes.

FACTS FACTS FACTS

Its name derives from the Dutch word koekje which means little cake. Cookies were first made from little pieces of cake batter that were cooked separately in order to test oven temperature.

Berry Smoothie

1 can crushed pineapple in juice, undrained
1 can blueberries in light syrup, drained
3 1/2 dl (1 1/2 cups) ice cubes
1 container lemon yogurt

Combine all ingredients in a blender, process until smooth.
Serve immediately.

TRIVIA TRIVIA TRIVIA

Barry White was the model for the character of "Chef" in the cartoon series
South Park. He was offered the role, but declined. As a devout Christian,
White was uncomfortable with South Park's often irreverent humor.
Isaac Hayes took the part instead.

Fruit Smoothie

1 package frozen mixed berries
1 can sliced peaches, drained
2 tbsp honey

In a blender, combine frozen fruit, canned fruit and honey.
Blend until smooth.

QUOTES QUOTES QUOTES

"-You are a smooth smoothie, you know."

-Fargo

The Good Smoothie

1 dl (1/2 cup) milk
1 dl (1/2 cup) plain yogurt
1/2 frozen banana, peeled and chopped
2 tbsp powdered protein powder
1 1/2 tbsp flax seed
1 tsp honey
1 dl (1/2 cup) frozen strawberries

In a blender, combine all ingredients.
Blend until smooth.

FACTS FACTS FACTS

Smooth operator is a generic term for any low-pass filter operation which smoothes a time function. In its simplest form, the running average over a number of samples in a time function is computed, an operation also known as box-car filtering. In finance, three-point or five-point windows are often used to flatten out fluctuations in financial data.

Healthy Fruit Smoothie

2 1/2 dl (1 cup) strawberries
1 dl (1/3 cup) frozen blueberries
2 bananas
1 dl (1/2 cup) orange juice
3 1/2 dl (1 1/2 cups) plain yogurt
1 tbsp soy milk powder

In a blender, combine all ingredients. Blend until smooth.

QUOTES QUOTES QUOTES

"-A lifetime of working with nuclear power has left me with a healthy green
glow... and left me as impotent as a Nevada boxing commissioner."
-The Simpsons

Banana Anna

1 banana
3 1/2 dl (1 1/2 cups) milk
1 tbsp honey
1/4 tsp ground nutmeg

In a blender, combine all ingredients. Blend until smooth.

QUOTES QUOTES QUOTES

"-I wonder about things, like, if they call an orange an 'orange' then why
don't we call a banana a 'yellow' or an apple a 'red'? Blueberries,
I understand. But will someone explain gooseberries to me?"
-Taxi

Smoothie Californique

7 large strawberries
1 container lemon yogurt
1 dl (1/3 cup) orange juice

Place strawberries in a plastic container and freeze for about an hour. When strawberries are frozen, combine all ingredients in a blender. Blend until smooth.

FACTS FACTS FACTS

Belvedere, Marin County, California, is not only the highest income city in California, judged by average per capita annual income of $113,595, but the highest income place in the U.S. (with a population over 1000).

Hawaii Smoothie

1 banana, chopped
1 can pineapple juice
3 tbsp coconut milk
1 tbsp white sugar

In a blender, combine all ingredients. Blend until smooth.

QUOTES QUOTES QUOTES

"-Hawaii is one of those places that keeps topping itself - just when you think you'll never see a sunset as beautiful, there comes a sunrise that even Gauguin can only imagine. It kind of makes unemployment easier to take."

-Magnum, P.I.

Crazy Good
Blueberry Muffins

1 dl (1/2 cup) butter
3 dl (1 1/4 cups) sugar
1/2 tsp salt
2 eggs
5 dl (2 cups) all-purpose flour, divided
2 tsp baking powder
1 dl (1/2 cup) buttermilk
4 1/2 dl (1 pint) fresh blueberries
2 tbsp sugar
Muffin cups

Preheat oven to 375 degrees F (190 degrees C).
In a large bowl, combine the butter, sugar and salt until light and fluffy. Beat in eggs one at a time. In a separate container, mix together 4 dl (1 3/4 cup) of the flour and baking powder. Beat this flour mixture alternately with the buttermilk, mixing just until incorporated. Crush 1/4 of the blueberries, and stir into the batter. Mix the rest of the whole blueberries with the remaining 1 dl (1/4 cup) of the flour, and fold into the batter. Scoop into muffin cups. Sprinkle tops lightly with sugar.
Bake in oven for 30 minutes, or until golden brown.

TRIVIA TRIVIA TRIVIA

Maine is the largest producer of Lowbush Blueberries in the U.S.. The annual Maine crop requires about 50,000 beehives for pollination, with most of the hives being trucked in from other states for that purpose.

Blueberry Pancakes

3 dl (1 1/4 cups) all-purpose flour
1/2 tsp salt
1 tbsp baking powder
1 1/4 tsp sugar
1 egg
2 1/2 dl (1 cup) milk
1/2 tbsp butter, melted
1 dl (1/2 cup) blueberries

In a large bowl, sift together flour, salt, baking powder and sugar.
In a separate bowl, beat together egg and milk. Stir milk and egg
into flour mixture. Mix in the butter and fold in the blueberries. Set
aside for 1 hour. Using 1/2 dl (1/4 cup) for each pancake, brown
on both sides in a frying pan.

FACTS FACTS FACTS

In Russia, Poland and Ukraine, the pancake-like blintz and blini are made
from wheat or buckwheat flour, yeast, butter, eggs and milk.

In Ethiopia, injera is made from a fermented sourdough batter of
buckwheat or the more traditional teff.

In Hungary, palacsinta are made from flour, milk, sugar, and eggs.
They are served as a main dish or as a dessert,
depending on the filling.

Apple Pie

1/2 dl (1/4 cup) light brown sugar
1/2 dl (1/4 cup) white sugar
1 tbsp all-purpose flour
1 tsp lemon juice
1/4 tsp ground cinnamon
9 dl (4 cups) peeled and pared apples
1 dl (1/2 cup) raisins
1 (23 cm / 9 inch) pie crusts
1 egg

Preheat oven to 425 degrees F (220 degrees C). Combine white sugar, light brown sugar, flour, lemon, cinnamon, and mix well. Add apples and raisins to sugar mixture and stir until fruit is well coated. Spoon apple mixture into pie crust. Place second piecrust on top of filling, and trim edges. Lightly glaze top of pie with a beaten egg, then sprinkle with a little sugar.
Bake till golden brown, about 35 to 40 minutes.
Let cool before serving.

QUOTES QUOTES QUOTES

"-Guys, uh, what exactly does third base feel like?
-You want to take this one?
-Like warm apple pie."

-American Pie

Swedish Pancakes
(a.k.a. Blondes of Sweden)

3 eggs
6 dl (2 1/2 cups) milk
3 dl (1 1/4 cup) flour
1 tbsp sugar
1/2 tsp salt
Butter

Combine all ingredients in a bowl until smooth.
Lightly butter a heated skillet and pour 1 dl (1/2 cup) of the butter into it. Swirl the pan with batter to expand to a thin layer. Cook until bubbles form and the pancake is golden brown on the bottom, about 1-1/2 minutes. Flip turn and continue to cook for about one more minute.
Butter skillet before frying the next pancake.
Serve with lingonberries.

FUN FUN FUN

The Swedish Bikini Team was a group of models who appeared in an advertising campaign for Old Milwaukee beer that ran for several months in 1991 in the United States. A group of men were bored or thirsty, then "saved" by the Swedish Bikini Team. The advertisements were dropped after protests by the National Organization of Women.

Elvis Sandwich

2 ripe bananas
1/2 dl (1/4 cup) creamy peanut butter
10 slices white sandwich bread
Butter...lots of it

Blend peanut butter with two ripe bananas until the mixture is creamy smooth. Spread on five slices of buttered bread. Top with remaining five slices. Place sandwiches in hot frying pan, in which several pats of butter have been melted. Cook until bread is lightly toasted, then flip over and cook the other side.

TRIVIA TRIVIA TRIVIA

Elvis sightings are a recurring phenomenon in which people claim to see American singer and rock star Elvis Presley, who is reported to have died in August 1977. There is an official Elvis Sighting Society which makes its World Headquarters at the Newport Restaurant in the Westboro section of Ottawa, Ontario.

Sightings of Elvis in the Yukon Territory are completely believable, since "Tagish" Elvis Presley, a local resident, has not only legally adopted the name, but dresses as Elvis and believes he is the late singer's reincarnation.

Drinks

Don't drink and drive

A Southern Screw

6 cl (2 oz) vodka
6 cl (2 oz) Southern Comfort
18 cl (6 oz) orange juice
Ice

Pour all ingredients over ice, stir and serve.

FACTS FACTS FACTS

In antiquity, the Greek mathematician Archytas of Tarentum
(428 – 350 BC) was credited with the invention of the screw.

A Piece of Ass

1 shot amaretto
1 shot Southern Comfort
Ice cubes
Sour mix to taste.

Pour all shots in an ice-filled glass. Fill with sour mix and serve.

TRIVIA TRIVIA TRIVIA

"Wild ass" may mean the wild donkey, or it may mean its wild relative
the onager, also known as a "half ass" - animal of the horse family.

The A-Rock

1/3 Spiced rum
1/3 Jack Daniels
1/3 Southern Comfort

Pour all ingredients into a chilled glass in the following order: start with rum,
then JD, and finally SoCo.

QUOTES QUOTES QUOTES

"-I thought you weren't crazy no more?
-Only on paper."

-The A-Team

Acapulco

4,5 cl (1 1/2 oz) tequila
1,5 cl (1/2 oz) triple sec
1,5 cl (1/2 oz) rum
Splash of lime juice
Splash of sour mix
Lime wedge

Shake all ingredients with ice, in a shaker.
Strain into a chilled cocktail glass,
or over fresh ice in a highball glass. Serve.

FACTS FACTS FACTS

'Old Blue Eyes' Frank Sinatra gave Acapulco a mention
in his all time classic Come Fly With Me.

Adios Motherfucker

1,5 cl (1/2 oz) vodka
1,5 cl (1/2 oz) rum
1,5 cl (1/2 oz) tequila
1,5 cl (1/2 oz)gin
1,5 cl (1/2 oz) Blue Curacao
6 cl (2 oz) sour mix
6 cl (2 oz) 7-Up

Pour all ingredients but the 7-Up into a chilled glass
filled with ice. Top with 7-Up and stir gently before serving.

TRIVIA TRIVIA TRIVIA

Many consider "motherfucker" to be one of the most offensive
profanities in the English language. A study published in
2000 found that British people consider it second
only to "cunt" in severity.

Agent Orange

3 cl (1 oz) vodka
1,5 cl (1/2 oz) Grand Marnier
1 cl (1/4 oz) Triple Sec
Splash of orange juice

Blend all ingredients with ice and serve in a highball glass.

FACTS FACTS FACTS

During the Vietnam War, the U.S. instituted a massive herbicidal program
with the aim to destroy the "cover" provided by the jungle-like forest,
and to deny food to the enemy. A variety of chemicals, fifteen in
total, were used operationally during this program, one of
them being Agent Orange.

Alien Secretion

1 cl (1/3 oz) vodka
1 cl (1/3 oz)Midori & Malibu
1 cl (1/3 oz) or a splash of pineapple juice (to taste)

Shake all ingredients together with ice and strain into a chilled cocktail glass or serve on the rocks.

QUOTES QUOTES QUOTES

"-I'm an alien, from the planet Melmac.
I have powers you can only dream of."

-ALF

All Jacked up

1,5 cl (1/2 oz) Jack Daniels
1 cl (1/3 oz) Sloe gin
1 cl (1/3 oz) melon liqueur
1 cl (1/3 oz) pineapple juice

Chill all ingredients in a mixing tin and pour.

QUOTES QUOTES QUOTES

"-He was jacked up higher than a prom dress in June."

-Death to Smoochy

B-52

1/3 Kahlua
1/3 Bailey's Irish Cream
1/3 Grand Marnier

Layer equal parts of each ingredient, in the order given, into a pony or shot glass. Alternatively, shake with ice and strain into a small rocks or chilled cocktail glass.

TRIVIA TRIVIA TRIVIA

Among its crew, the B-52 is affectionately known as the "BUFF", an acronym for "Big Ugly Fat Fucker". During the Cold War, the United States Air Force always kept part of their fleet of B-52s airborne to launch a nuclear attack on the Soviet Union if necessary.

Baby, Baby, Baby

3 cl (1 oz) vodka
2,5 cl (3/4 oz) Grand Marnier
1,5 cl (1/2 oz) Baileys

Hand swirl all ingredients over ice.
Strain into a chilled cocktail glass and serve.

QUOTES QUOTES QUOTES

"-Nobody puts Baby in a corner."

-Dirty Dancing

Bahama Mama

4,5 cl (1 1/2 oz) coconut rum
1,5 cl (1/2 oz) triple sec
splash of cream of coconut
splash of pineapple juice
dash of Grenadine
whipped cream
orange slice
Maraschino cherry

Shake juice and liquor with ice.
Strain into a chilled cocktail glass
or over fresh ice in a highball glass.
Add a topping of whipped cream and a cherry, and serve.

FACTS FACTS FACTS

Christopher Columbus's first landfall in the New World in 1492 is
believed to have been on the island of San Salvador,
in the southeastern Bahamas.

Black Russian

4,5 cl (1 1/2 oz) vodka
2,5 cl (3/4 oz) Kahlua

Mix vodka and Kahlua over ice in a rocks glass, and serve.

QUOTES QUOTES QUOTES

"-Russian police. Stern. Stern, but fair."

-Jackass

Blue Lagoon

3 cl (1 oz) Malibu rum
pineapple juice
1,5 cl (1/2 oz) blue curacao

Mix Malibu rum and pineapple juice in a highball
or collins glass. Float blue curacao on top, and serve.

Bloody Mary

4,5 cl (1 1/2 oz) vodka
dash of Worcestershire sauce
dash of Tabasco sauce
dash of lemon juice
celery salt
pepper
tomato juice

Pour spices over ice in a tall glass, then add vodka.
Fill with tomato juice & stir.
Garnish with a celery stick and a lime wedge before serving.

FACTS FACTS FACTS

Mary I, also known as Mary Tudor, was Queen of England and Queen
of Ireland from 6 July 1553 until her death. Mary had almost three
hundred religious dissenters executed. As a consequence,
she is often known as Bloody Mary.

Brass Monkey

1,5 cl (1/2 oz) rum
1,5 cl (1/2 oz) vodka
12 cl (4 oz) orange juice

Mix rum and vodka and stir gently. Add orange juice and shake well. Pour over ice in a large glass.

TRIVIA TRIVIA TRIVIA

The phrase "cold enough to freeze the balls off a brass monkey" is sometimes used by English speakers. However, nobody knows what a brass monkey refers to.

Cactus Bowl

27 cl (9 oz) pineapple juice
18 cl (6 oz) lime juice
9 cl (3 oz) light rum
4,5 cl (1 1/2 oz) spiced rum
4,5 cl (1 1/2 oz) amaretto

Mix all ingredients with ice.
Pour into a margarita glass and serve on the rocks.

FACTS FACTS FACTS

In the months leading up to Super Bowl XXX (or Super Bowl Thirty), some proxy servers were blocking the web site for the upcoming event. Many proxy servers' filters were configured to block the text string "XXX" whenever occurring to prevent access to pornography.

Californian

4 cl (1 1/4 oz) vodka
splash of grapefruit juice
splash of orange juice

Mix all ingredients and pour over ice in a highball glass.

QUOTES QUOTES QUOTES

"-Reebs. That's what we used to call them when we was kids.
It's beer spelled backwards."

-Kalifornia

Freddy Kruger

1/3 sambuca
1/3 Jägermeister
1/3 vodka

Layer equal parts of each ingredient, in order given,
into a pony or shot glass. Serve.

Cement Mixer

4 cl (1 1/4 oz) Bailey's Irish Cream
2,5 cl (3/4 oz) Rose's lime juice

Chill Bailey's and strain into shot glass. Pour lime juice
in another glass. Take the Bailey's into your mouth,
without swallowing. Follow with the lime juice
and swirl in mouth before swallowing.

TRIVIA TRIVIA TRIVIA

Over 55,000 miles of freeways and highways in America are
made of concrete. An old name for it is liquid stone.

Cosmopolitan

3 cl (1 oz) vodka
1,5 cl (1/2 oz) triple sec
1,5 cl (1/2 oz) Rose's sweetened lime juice
1,5 cl (1/2 oz) cranberry juice
lime wedge

Shake all ingredients in a shaker with ice.
Serve in a martini glass garnished with a lime wedge.

FACTS FACTS FACTS

The Cosmopolitan Resort & Casino opens, just south of the Bellagio, in mid
2008. The $1.8 billion project will feature 2,000 condominiums, 1,000
hotel rooms, a 75,000 sq ft casino, 300,000 sq ft of retail, restaurant and
entertainment space, and 150,000 sq ft of meeting/convention space.

Cuba Libre

4 cl (1 1/4 oz) rum
Coca Cola
dash of lime juice
lime wedge

Mix all ingredients over ice in a highball glass.
Garnish with a lime wedge and serve.

FACTS FACTS FACTS

The Cuba Libre was invented in Havana, Cuba around 1900. Patriots
aiding Cuba during the Spanish-American War regularly mixed rum
and Coca-Cola as a cocktail and a toast to this West Indies island.

Dirty Harry

3 cl (1 oz) Grand Marnier
3 cl (1 oz) Tia Maria

Shake all ingredients over ice. Strain into a chilled cocktail
glass or build over ice in a rocks glass before serving.

QUOTES QUOTES QUOTES

"-I know what you're thinking. "Did he fire six shots or only five?" Well, to tell
you the truth, in all this excitement I kind of lost track myself. But being as
this is a .44 Magnum, the most powerful handgun in the world, and would
blow your head clean off, you've got to ask yourself a question: Do I feel
lucky? Well, do ya, punk?"

-Dirty Harry

E.T.

1/3 Midori
1/3 Bailey's Irish Cream
1/3 vodka

Layer equal parts of each ingredient, in the order given, into a pony or shot glass. Phone home.

QUOTES QUOTES QUOTES

"-He's a man from outer space and we're taking him to his spaceship.
Well, can't he just beam up?
-This is REALITY, Greg."

-E.T.

Fire and Ice

1/3 Sambuca
1/3 Triple Sec
1/3 brandy

Stir all ingredients with ice in a lowball glass.

Fuzzy Navel

4,5 cl (1 1/2 oz) Peach schnapps
orange juice to taste

Pour peach schnapps into ice-filled collins glass.
Fill with orange juice and stir to combine.

FUN FUN FUN

The Fuzzy Duck Drinking Game:
In turn, players alternately utter the phrases "fuzzy duck" and "ducky fuzz".
A player may also opt to say, "does he?" in which case play resumes
in the opposite direction. If a player says the wrong thing, plays out of
turn, says "does he" too often, or breaks the rhythm of the game,
'they have to drink.

Gin and Tonic

6 cl (2 oz) gin
9 cl (3 oz) tonic water

Pour the gin and tonic water into a lowball glass almost
filled with ice. Stir well. Garnish with a lime wedge.

TRIVIA TRIVIA TRIVIA

In the Hitchhiker's Guide to the Galaxy series, it is stated that each race
in the galaxy has developed a drink that is pronounced the same, but
spelled differently (such as jynantonnyx). The reason for this is one of
the great mysteries of the universe.

Gremlin

4,5 cl (1 1/2 oz) vodka
2,5 cl (3/4 oz) Blue Curacao
2,5 cl (3/4 oz) rum
splash of orange juice

Shake all ingredients with ice & strain into a chilled cocktail glass. Don't serve it after midnight.

QUOTES QUOTES QUOTES

"-Bright light! Bright light!"

-Gremlins

Hurricane

4,5 cl (1 1/2 oz) light rum
4,5 cl (1 1/2 oz)dark rum
3 cl (1 oz) passion fruit syrup
2,5 cl (3/4 oz) lime juice

Shake all ingredients with ice and serve in a hurricane glass.

QUOTES QUOTES QUOTES

"-Hate put me in prison. Love's gonna bust me out. "

-The Hurricane

Harvey Wallbanger

4 cl (1 1/4 oz) vodka
float of Galliano liqueur
orange juice

Mix vodka and orange juice over ice in a tall glass.
Float Galliano on top and serve.

TRIVIA TRIVIA TRIVIA

The Harvey Wallbanger cocktail was invented in Los Angeles during the
1950's. Harvey was actually a Californian surfer. After losing an important
contest, he consoled himself in Duke's Blackwatch bar with one of his
'special' screwdriver cocktails. After several drinks, he tried to leave the
bar, but kept bumping into the furniture and walls. Harvey 'the Wallbanger'
became his nickname and the famous drink was named.

Jäger Tonic

4 cl (1 1/4 oz) Jägermeister
tonic water

Pour Jägermeister over ice in a highball glass.
Fill with tonic water and garnish with an orange
slice before serving.

Kamikaze

3 cl (1 oz) vodka
2,5 cl (3/4 oz) triple sec
dash of lime juice
splash of sour mix

Shake all ingredients over ice.
Strain into a chilled cocktail,
pony or shot glass and serve.

FACTS FACTS FACTS

In the Japanese language, Kamikaze is translated as "Divine wind".
It came into being as the name of a legendary typhoon said to
have saved Japan from a Mongol invasion fleet in 1281.

Lava Flow

3 cl (1 oz) light rum
3 cl (1 oz) Malibu rum
6 cl (2 oz) strawberries
1 banana
6 cl (2 oz) pineapple juice
6 cl (2 oz) coconut cream

Blend banana, coconut cream, and pineapple juice in
a blender and set aside. In bottom of hurricane glass,
stir together both rums and strawberries.
Pour banana/coconut/pineapple mix
into glass slowly while serving.

FACTS FACTS FACTS

The lava lamp will not work until the liquid is sufficiently warmed by the
lamp. On November 30, 2004, 24-year-old Philip Quinn died in a
lava lamp accident. The glass lamp bottle exploded while Mr.
Quinn was heating it on top of his home stove, killing him
by sending a glass shard through his heart.

Lobotomy

1/3 amaretto
1/3 Chambord
1/3 pineapple juice
champagne

Shake equal parts of the first three ingredients over ice.
Strain into a chilled cocktail, pony or shot glass.
Top with champagne and serve.

TRIVIA TRIVIA TRIVIA

The first human lobotomy was performed by Antonio Egas Moniz in 1936.
He won the Nobel Prize for medicine in 1949 for this work.
The procedure was popularized in the United States by Dr. Walter Freeman,
who traveled the country performing 'ice pick lobotomies' on patients with
psychiatric disorders. Eventually he began performing this procedure on
anyone who wished to have one.

Long Island Iced Tea

1/5 vodka
1/5 tequila
1/5 rum
1/5 gin
1/5 triple sec
splash of Sour mix
splash Coca Cola
Mix all ingredients over ice in a glass. Pour into shaker and give one brisk shake. Pour back into glass and garnish with lemon.

FACTS FACTS FACTS

Because of strict liquor laws in Utah, a Long Island Iced Tea must be served there in five shot glasses with the soda, sour and ice in a separate glass, or a single glass with a single shot of alcohol with the 'flavors' of the other liquors.

Mai Tai

3 cl (1 oz) Martinique Rum
3 cl (1 oz) Ja
1,5 cl (1/2 oz) Orange curacao
1 cl (1/4 oz) Rock Candy syrup
1 cl (1/4 oz) Orgeat syrup
fresh lime

Squeeze lime over ice, add remaining ingredients
And shaved ice. Hand shake & serve in a double old
fashioned glass. Garnish with a 1/2 of the lime shell
& fresh mint sprig.

FUN FUN FUN

"Maitai" is the Tahitian word for "good."

Manhattan

4,5 cl (1 1/2 oz) whiskey or bourbon
2,5 cl (3/4 oz) sweet vermouth
dash of Bitters

Mix all ingredients in a rocks glass, or stir over ice and strain into a chilled cocktail glass. Garnish with a lemon twist and serve.

QUOTES QUOTES QUOTES

"-Is your vagina listed in the New York City guide books?
Because it should be - hottest spot in town. Always open."

-Sex and the City

Margarita

4,5 cl (1 1/2 oz) tequila
2,5 cl (3/4 oz) triple sec (or Cointreau)
splash of Sour mix
dash of fresh lime juice

Shake all ingredients with ice & serve in a salt rimmed glass on the rocks.

FUN FUN FUN

"Margaritaville" is a 1977 song by Jimmy Buffett. The song topped the Billboard charts at No. 1 in the "Adult Contemporary" category and at No. 8 for "Pop Singles."

Martini

4,5 cl (1 1/2 oz) gin
2,5 cl (3/4 oz) dry vermouth
one olive

Stir gin and vermouth over ice cubes in a mixing glass.
Strain into a cocktail glass, add the olive, and serve.

QUOTES QUOTES QUOTES

"-A martini. Shaken, not stirred."

-Goldfinger

Mojito

4 cl (1 1/4 oz) rum
splash of soda
dash of simple syrup
mint

Mix mint leaves with simple syrup, add ice, rum
& top with soda. Garnish with a sprig of fresh mint.

FACTS FACTS FACTS

On April 26, 2004, the Buena Vista Township Committee voted to tempo-
rarily rename the community of Richland, a section of Buena Vista
Township. For the first half of the month of May, Richland became Mojito,
New Jersey, named after the Cuban rum drink. Bacardi had offered to
give the township $5,000 for recreation projects in exchange for a sign
placed on U.S. Highway 40.

Orange Crush

1/3 vodka
1/3 triple sec
1/3 orange juice

Shake equal parts of each ingredient over ice.
Strain into a chilled cocktail, pony or shot glass and serve.

TRIVIA TRIVIA TRIVIA

Orange Crush was invented by J. M. Thompson of Chicago in 1906.

Pac Man

1/3 Bitters
1/3 Grenadine
1/3 ginger ale
splash of lemon juice

Stir all but ginger ale over ice. Fill with ginger ale,
garnish with an orange slice and serve.

QUOTES QUOTES QUOTES

"-Richie loved to use 22s because the bullets are small and they don't
come out the other end like a 45, see, a 45 will blow a barn door out the
back of your head and there's a lot of dry cleaning involved, but a 22 will
just rattle around like Pac-Man until you're dead."

-My Blue Heaven

Popped Cherry

1,5 cl (1/2 oz) vodka
1,5 cl (1/2 oz) raspberry schnapps
cranberry juice
club soda
1 cherry

Stir vodka and rasberry schnapps with ice.
Fill with cranberry juice and top with club soda.
Garnish with cherry with a slice in it.

QUOTES QUOTES QUOTES

"-Popped your boardroom cherry. Isn't that great?"

-The Apprentice

Roadrunner Punch

1/3 Malibu rum
1/3 Blue Curacao
1/3 Peach schnapps
fruit punch

Mix all the alcohol in a large glass with ice.
Top off with fruit punch and serve. Beep-beep!!

TRIVIA TRIVIA

The current Guinness World Records for 428 punches a minute and 9
punches a second were set in September 2005 by Robert Ardito, a
student of Grandmaster Jim Fung's International Wing Chun Academy.

Sangria

1 1/2 L red wine
2 1/2 dl (1 cup / 24 cl) sugar
1 large lemon, sliced
1 large orange, sliced
1 large apple, cut into thin sections
12 cl (4 oz) brandy
soda water

Mix wine, sugar and fruit and let it sit in the fridge for
18-24 hours, or until it has a syrupy consistency. Before serving,
stir in brandy and cut the with soda water until it has a wine like
consistency.
Serve from a pitcher in wine glasses.

FACTS FACTS FACTS

Sangria was introduced to the American public when it was featured at
the Spanish Pavilion of the 1964 New York World's Fair.

Rusty Nail

3 cl (1 oz) Scotch
3 cl (1 oz) Drambuie

Mix & serve on the rocks.

Scooby Snack

1/3 Midori
1/3 Malibu rum
1/3 1/2 & 1/2
splash of pineapple juice

Shake all ingredients with ice and pour into a tumbler.

QUOTES QUOTES QUOTES

"-Who's your best buddy?
-Raggy!
-That's right. And who's my best buddy in the whole wide world?
-Rooby Doo!"

-Scooby-Doo

Screwdriver

4 cl (1 1/4 oz) vodka
orange juice

Mix over ice in a highball glass.

Seabreeze

4 cl (1 1/4 oz) vodka
grapefruit Juice
cranberry Juice

Mix and serve over ice in a highball glass.

QUOTES QUOTES QUOTES

"-The concept of this video is: I'm so hot, everyone
wants to screw me, and that's pretty much it."

-The Andy Dick Show

Sex on the Beach

3 cl (1 oz) vodka
2,5 cl (3/4 oz) Peach schnapps
cranberry juice
grapefruit juice

Half fill a highball glass with cranberry juice and
grapefruit juice, stir in vodka and peach schnapps and serve.

FACTS FACTS FACTS

In zoology, a hermaphrodite is an organism of a species whose members
possess both male and female sexual organs during their lives.

Singapore Sling

4 cl (1 1/4 oz) gin
dash of Grenadine
Sour mix
soda
dash of cherry brandy

Shake gin, Grenadine & sour mix together and pour in large glass.
Add a splash of soda and float cherry brandy on top.
Garnish with an orange slice and a cherry and serve.

TRIVIA TRIVIA TRIVIA

The Singapore Sling was invented by Mr. Ngiam Tong Boon for the Raffles
Hotel in Singapore sometime between 1910 and 1915. At one point the
recipe was forgotten by the bar staff. The recipe currently used by the
hotel was the result of recreating the original recipe based on the
memories of former bartenders.

Tequila Sunrise

4,5 cl (1 1/2 oz) tequila
orange juice
dash of Grenadine

Mix all ingredients over ice in a collins or tall glass.
Trickle grenadine so it falls through the drink, like a lava lamp.

QUOTES QUOTES QUOTES

"-Don't worry, buddy. I won't kill her unless you approve.
-And if I don't approve?
-Then we'll talk until you do."

-Tequila Sunrise

Vodka Martini

4,5 cl (1 1/2 oz) vodka
2,5 cl (3/4 oz) dry vermouth
one olive

Shake the vodka and vermouth together with ice.
Strain into a cocktail glass, add the olive and serve.

QUOTES QUOTES QUOTES

"-If God wanted me on ice, he would have made me a vodka martini."

-Queer as Folk

Warm Blonde

1/2 Southern Comfort
1/2 amaretto

Layer amaretto and Southern Comfort
in a pony or shot glass and serve.

FUN FUN FUN

A blonde, wanting to earn some money, decided to hire herself out as
a handyman-type and started canvassing a wealthy neighborhood.
She went to the front door of the first house and asked the owner if he had
any jobs for her to do. "Well, you can paint my porch. How much will you
charge?" The blonde said, "How about 50 dollars?" The man agreed
and told her that the paint and ladders that she might need were in the
garage. The man's wife, inside the house, heard the conversation and said
to her husband, "Does she realize that the porch goes all the way around
the house?" The man replied, "She should. She was standing on the porch."
A short time later, the blonde came to the door to collect her money.
"You're finished already?" he asked. "Yes," the blonde answered,
"and I had paint left over, so I gave it two coats. "Impressed, the man
reached in his pocket for the $50. "And by the way," the blonde added,
"that's not a Porch, it's a Ferrari."

White Russian

4 cl (1 1/4 oz) vodka
3 cl (1 oz) Kahlua
splash of cream

Shake ingredients together and serve over ice in a highball glass.

QUOTES QUOTES QUOTES

"-White Russian, no ice, no vodka... hold the Kahlua."

-Catwoman

Zombie

6 cl (2 oz) light rum
3 cl (1 oz) dark rum
3 cl (1 oz) Apricot brandy
splash simple syrup
pineapple juice
dash of 151 Rum

Blend rums, brandy, simple syrup & pineapple juice
with ice. Pour into a collins or hurricane glass and
float 151 on top before serving.

FACTS FACTS FACTS

According to the tenets of voodoo, a dead person can be revived by a
houngan or mambo. After resurrection, it has no will of its own, but remains
under the control of the person who performed the ritual. Such resurrected
dead are called "zombies".

www.nicotext.com

www.nicotext.com

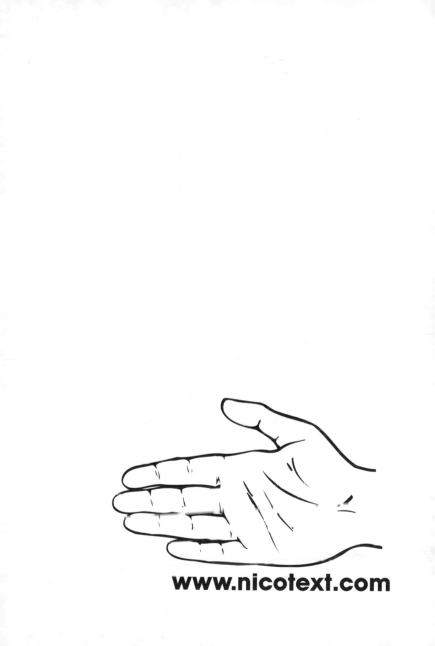

www.nicotext.com

NICOTEXT wants YOU!

This is what I liked with this book:

This is what I didn't like with this book:

I want a catalogue (your adress) :

I want to receive an email now and then (your email):

My friend wants a catalogue (friends address):

I want a million dollars: ☐ yes ☐ no

Next time, why don't you make a book about:

Tear and send to: NICOTEXT, Box 9020, 503 19 Boras, Sweden